TRISH DESEINE

French Country Cooking

RECIPES & TABLE SETTINGS FOR ALL SEASONS

photography
Joann Pai

KYLE BOOKS

TRISH DESEINE

French Country Cooking

photography
Joann Pai

Preface

French cuisine is a little like New York City in the way it now exists in our collective consciousness. Even if we have never physically experienced it in France ourselves, we feel we know it. It's familiar, comforting and woven oh so lightly into our memories, real or imagined. As for French country cooking, it is perhaps more a state of mind than a specific set of instructions set in a certain time or place. Obviously, acquiring that mindset is easier if you are in France, as I have been for over 35 years – immersed in its vast, diverse food culture and landscapes, with access to all the wonderful ingredients and advice I'm lucky enough to take for granted. But even if you're reading this in a city on the other side of the world, there's nothing to stop you giving your menu and dining table a French countryside ambience. It's really very easy! All it takes is a slightly wilted bouquet of old roses or dahlias whose petals fall prettily on the table, a few lovely, mismatched pieces of crockery (late 19th-century French terre de fer if you can track some down), bread in a basket (but no bread plates), and a linen sheet in place of a tablecloth to give it that bucolic touch à la George Sand in her exquisite yet lively and food-loving country house in Nohant, south of the Loire valley. Then, the food you serve up should be comforting, traditional, verging on nostalgic and prepared as much as you can from fresh, seasonal farm produce (the all-important terroir in French cuisine). I recently heard a super-chic Parisian hostess say that her guests' favourite dinners were the ones that reminded them of their childhood – soups, purées, stews and chocolate mousse for a 'baby food' effect. Without taking it quite that far, it is reassuring to know that this high-low contrast between a sophisticated table setting and a very simple menu can be part of the pleasure of entertaining, for both host and guests.

Introduction

In France, with its quasi-religious love and respect for holidays and leisure time at weekends, and easy access to rich and diverse rural landscapes and culinary traditions, we all have memories of lunches in the countryside. It might have been as children at our grandparents' house, or as adults in a country cottage rented for a weekend, the holidays, or borrowed from some generous friends, or even better – our own!

More than ever, the countryside evokes visions of a quiet and simple life, where everything feels more liberating and closer to nature. However, nowadays we are also hyper-aware that behind the dream of a bucolic countryside, as depicted in the Impressionist paintings of Monet, Pissarro and Manet – although possible for the duration of a classic long French lunch – lies a much harsher reality. We are (thankfully) becoming more tuned into the fragility of the planet and the efforts of eco-warriors to protect it, as well as those of the farmers who struggle to make ends meet while doing their best to feed us in a healthy, ethical and sustainable way.

So it is against this backdrop of modern reality that I set this vision of a 'perfect' lunch and traditional, slightly nostalgic French recipes that follow. Despite the somewhat romantic, idealized settings and table decor, I've tried to come up with easy, super-practical recipes. Just like most of the French cooks I've learned from over the years, I promise you won't be toiling away alone in the kitchen for days on end just for a few fleeting moments of culinary pleasure.

In my French country kitchen, I find everything that happens before and after time spent around the table is just as important and pleasureful. The planning of the menu and setting, the buying and picking of ingredients – especially if you are lucky enough to have access to a garden and to local markets and producers – and the moments you spend preparing the feast, hopefully with others around you pitching in. There is always plenty to look forward to besides the meal itself: peeling and hulling fruit and vegetables with the kids, shucking oysters with friends, choosing the wine, slicing the baguettes, fireside games, lazy-hazy naps in the shade, followed by walks in the forest or over the fields with everyone, and lots more.

The book offers menu suggestions based on different French seasons and occasions, with two distinct versions for summer – one for our early summer, featuring crisp, bright, early-season produce, such as asparagus, new vegetables and first strawberries, and one for high summer, featuring sun-soaked tomatoes, pungent melons and a general abundance of all fruit and vegetables. These are the months of the year when we entertain most in the countryside, with prettily laid tables in the garden. Personally, though, I much prefer a cosy autumnal meal indoors, before wrapping up warm to go for a stroll in the fresh air or a browse around my local antique shops for some interesting tableware.

I have included themed recipe sections on appetizers, salads, eggs, chicken, vegetables, cakes and tarts based on what can be found in a French country storecupboard and classic cookbooks. These are simple, versatile recipes that everyone loves, and are still served regularly, even if they can go in and out of fashion in other countries! I also hope you will be inspired by the table decor and settings, all created with my finds from brocante shops over the years.

As for my inspiration for this collection of recipes and table settings, it comes, as ever, from everything I have learned and adapted from the cooks and customs I've experienced since I first came to live in France. Then, in our Normandy family weekend home, an old cider press, the rickety table on wheels, carefully piled with dishes and cutlery, rolled noisily from the tiny kitchen over stone tiles to the main table – set next to the fire in autumn or by a window with a valley view in summer – and we still always managed to forget something vital in the kitchen! The often-rowdy lunches would regularly begin at noon with a glass of chilled white wine and end at four o'clock (or later) after naps under parasols or the catalpa or apple trees. The tables looked like still-life paintings to me, decorated in the colours of seasonal flowers, laid with a pretty tablecloth and old, but always polished, silverware.

Today, lunches like these, unapologetically, nostalgically, *à la Française*, are also an opportunity to dream of a healed planet, to get together and enjoy the food, in the company of others. In my mind, I see these occasions around a French table as wonderful time machines that can send us back to gentler years, while simultaneously creating lasting, happy memories for the future.

I hope you enjoy the recipes, and the ride.

Trish

Barbour
Barbour

It's apéritif time

Don't work too hard! Except perhaps at Christmas (but even then, don't overdo it). Banish those fancy canapés that need assembling at the last minute. Go for some easy options, be generous and let your guests help themselves as they circulate and chat. In France, it's the ideal opportunity to showcase local produce. We prefer local wines, ciders and juices. We treat ourselves (and everyone else) to produce from the charcuterie counter or the local butcher's – pâtés en croûte, rillettes, etc. – and prepare only the dips, pickles and crudités at home. And, as always, there's nothing to stop you from laying even the apéro the table beautifully with treasured finds from the flea market and a few seasonal flowers.

GNE
DSIECK

Cervelle de canut

SERVES 6–8
PREPARATION: 10 MINUTES

- 500g (1lb 2oz) fromage blanc (or use quark)
- 1 shallot, peeled and finely chopped
- 1 garlic clove, peeled and finely chopped
- 3 tablespoons chopped chives, plus extra to garnish
- 2 tablespoons red wine vinegar
- 3 tablespoons olive oil
- salt and pepper

This retro creamy, garlicky dip translates as 'canut brain' – a derogatory name questioning the intelligence of 19th-century Lyonnais silk weavers, les canuts.

- Put all the ingredients in a bowl and whisk to combine.
- Serve chilled, garnished with chives.

Provençal pistou

SERVES 6
PREPARATION: 5 MINUTES

- 2 garlic cloves, peeled
- 1 good-sized bunch of fresh basil, leaves picked
- 150ml (5fl oz) olive oil
- 2–3 tablespoons freshly grated Parmesan cheese
- salt and pepper

Unlike its close cousin, pesto, real French pistou doesn't have pine nuts in it. Parmesan is also optional, but I really like adding it to beef up the flavour and texture.

- Put the garlic and a good pinch of salt into a small mixer or, even better, a mortar, then grind it into a purée (using a pestle if necessary). Add the basil leaves, then grind in the oil and Parmesan alternately. Stir well before serving.

Classic tapenade

SERVES 6–8
PREPARATION: 2 MINUTES

- 200g (7oz) pitted black olives
- 1 garlic clove, peeled
- 1 tablespoon capers
- 5 salted anchovy fillets
- 3–4 tablespoons olive oil

There's nothing like this combination of salty ingredients to whet your appetite.

- Place all the ingredients in a small mixer and pulse to make a rough purée. For a more authentic result, you can also use a mortar and pestle.

Roquefort dip

SERVES 8
PREPARATION: 3 MINUTES

- 300g (10½oz) fromage blanc (or use crème fraîche or Greek yogurt)
- 100g (3½oz) Roquefort cheese
- salt and pepper

- Place all the ingredients in a bowl and mix well to incorporate the Roquefort into the fromage blanc. Leave a few small lumps to create some texture.

TIP
Serve direct from the refrigerator with small endive leaves for dipping.

Red onion pickles

FOR 1 LARGE JAR
PREPARATION: 10 MINUTES
STANDING: 2–3 HOURS

- 300ml (10fl oz) cider vinegar
- 6–7 coriander seeds
- 1 star anise
- 1 bay leaf
- 6–7 black peppercorns
- 3 tablespoons brown sugar
- 1 tablespoon sea salt flakes
- 3–4 red onions, peeled and sliced into rings

It's always good to have some of this condiment in the refrigerator to accompany your cheese and charcuterie platters.

- Place the vinegar, coriander, star anise, bay leaf, peppercorns, brown sugar and salt in a saucepan and bring to the boil. Stir to make sure the sugar has completely dissolved.
- Put the onions in a heatproof bowl and pour the boiling vinegar over them. Stir and leave to infuse for at least 2 or 3 hours.

TIP
The onions will keep very well for up to 2 weeks in the refrigerator.

Mackerel and salmon rillettes

SERVES 8
PREPARATION: 15 MINUTES

- 200g (7oz) smoked mackerel
- 200g (7oz) smoked salmon
- 300g (10½oz) spreadable cream cheese

FOR THE MACKEREL

- 2 tablespoons pink peppercorns, lightly crushed
- juice of ½ lemon

FOR THE SALMON

- 2 tablespoons chopped dill
- 1 tablespoon chopped chives
- 1 teaspoon grated lemon zest
- white pepper

TO GARNISH

- salmon roe
- chopped fresh herbs, such as dill or parsley

Two versions, one method. Always popular at my lunches and so easy to serve.

- Remove the flesh from the mackerel and flake it. Take care to remove all the bones.
- Slice the salmon into thin strips.
- Mix the mackerel with half of the cream cheese and stir in the pink peppercorns and lemon juice.
- Mix the rest of the cheese with the salmon, herbs and lemon zest. Season with white pepper.
- Place each mixture in a pretty bowl, garnish with salmon roe and fresh herbs, then serve.

Salads for all seasons

Here, my aim is to remind you of the richness of French heritage when it comes to salads. The low-end deli counters may have dulled our appetite and risked giving many salads a bad reputation, but they are truly delicious when prepared at home with good ingredients.

It's also a way to make menus more plant-based, so forget the meat and the dictates of food fashion, and brush up on your classics.

Piedmontese salad

SERVES 6–8
PREPARATION: 15 MINUTES

- 1kg (2lb 4oz) new potatoes, boiled and roughly chopped
- 4 hard-boiled eggs, cut into quarters
- about 10 gherkins, sliced into rounds
- 2 good firm tomatoes, chopped into 2cm (¾in) pieces
- 200g (7oz) piece of ham or ham hock, diced
- 1 small bunch of flat-leaf parsley, chopped, to garnish

FOR THE MAYONNAISE SAUCE

- 2 egg yolks
- 1 tablespoon Dijon mustard
- 1 tablespoon white wine or cider vinegar
- 250ml (9fl oz) sunflower oil
- 150ml (5fl oz) whipping cream
- salt and pepper

This poor salad's reputation has been almost ruined by industrial food producers. It's well worth making a great homemade version with good, fresh ingredients.

- Make the mayonnaise by whisking the egg yolks with the mustard, vinegar and just enough oil to emulsify, then continue whisking as you pour in the rest of the oil in a thin stream. Once you've got a nice, thick mayonnaise, add the cream to make a sauce. Season with salt and pepper.
- Place all the ingredients in a large salad bowl, pour in the sauce and stir gently.
- Garnish with chopped flat-leaf parsley and enjoy.

Frisée with Mimolette cheese and tarragon

SERVES 6–8
PREPARATION: 10 MINUTES

- 1 head of frisée (curly endive)
- 150g (5½oz) mature Mimolette cheese (or use Gouda or good-quality mature Cheddar, red in colour if possible)
- a few fresh tarragon leaves

FOR THE VINAIGRETTE

- 1 tablespoon tarragon vinegar
- 3 tablespoons neutral oil (grapeseed, rapeseed, etc.)
- salt and pepper

A blend of flavours inspired by the delightful menu at Bouchon Racine in London. This way of serving salad (and cheese) looks decorative on your table and makes your life easier.

- Separate the lettuce leaves. Wash and spin them, then place flat on a large plate.
- Cut the cheese into very thin slices and scatter them over the lettuce with the tarragon leaves.
- Prepare the vinaigrette by mixing one-third of the vinegar and two-thirds of the oil with a fork, until emulsified. Season to taste.
- Serve the salad tossed in the vinaigrette.

Green bean and hazelnut salad

SERVES 6
PREPARATION: 10 MINUTES
COOKING: 30 MINUTES

- 300g (10½oz) green beans
- 30g (1oz) shelled hazelnuts
- 2 tablespoons toasted hazelnut oil
- 2 teaspoons lemon juice
- salt and pepper
- curly parsley, chopped, to garnish

The hazelnuts toasted in the oil for the dressing totally transform this simple side dish. Serve cold or warm.

- Steam or boil the beans. They should stay crunchy. Drain and leave them to cool.
- Toast the hazelnuts in a dry frying pan or in the oven. Once they've browned, lightly crush them.
- Mix the oil with the lemon juice, salt and pepper. Combine the vinaigrette and hazelnuts with the green beans.
- Place on a large plate and garnish with parsley.

Eggs

Eggs, along with cheese, are among your best friends in classic French cookery. A beautiful quiche or cheese tart are lifesavers for a last-minute lunch, while soft-boiled eggs, served in pretty bric-a-brac egg cups with homemade flavoured butter, can make a delicious old-fashioned starter. Eggs meurette (poached eggs in red wine sauce) are so easy to make and, most importantly, can be prepared ahead of time. And finally, a piperade, served with one or two fresh seasonal salads and accompanied by some good cured ham, is a treat whatever the time of year.

Eggs meurette

SERVES 6
PREPARATION: 5–10 MINUTES
COOKING: 25 MINUTES

- 30g (1oz) butter
- 4–5 shallots, peeled and finely chopped
- 1 small onion, peeled and finely chopped
- 1 garlic clove, peeled and finely chopped
- 1 teaspoon cornflour
- 750ml (25fl oz) red wine
- 1 bouquet garni (bay leaf, thyme, rosemary)
- 6 eggs
- vinegar
- 150g (5½oz) bacon lardons
- salt and pepper

This dish of poached eggs served in a red wine sauce is rich and comforting. Add mushrooms to give it an even thicker consistency.

- Heat a knob of butter in a frying pan and sweat the shallots, onion and garlic for about 10 minutes, without letting them brown.
- Sprinkle in the cornflour and stir. Pour in the wine, add the bouquet garni and mix well with a wooden spoon.
- Leave to simmer and reduce over a low heat for about 20 minutes, until you obtain a thick, shiny sauce. Season with salt and pepper and set aside.
- Poach the eggs for around 3 minutes in boiling water with a drop of vinegar added. Drain them and trim if necessary to make a nice shape.
- Fry the bacon lardons and reheat the sauce. Mix together, then pour the sauce onto plates, and top each serving with an egg.

TIP
Serve with toasted bread.

Soft-boiled eggs, truffle butter and brioche

SERVES 6
PREPARATION: 15 MINUTES
COOKING: 5 MINUTES

- 180g (6oz) slightly salted butter, at room temperature
- 25g (1oz) black truffle, fresh if possible
- 6 fresh eggs
- 6 slices of brioche

You might already know how much I love butter, and here it's made doubly delicious – flavoured with fresh black truffle and spread generously on toasted brioche.

- Place the butter and truffle in a mini-blender and blend for a few seconds to make a speckled mixture.
- Soft-boil the eggs, toast the slices of brioche and serve hot with the butter spread on.

The real quiche Lorraine

SERVES 6–8
PREPARATION: 25 MINUTES
COOKING: 50 MINUTES
CHILLING: 2 HOURS

- 200g (7oz) piece of smoked pork belly or bacon
- 5 eggs, plus 3 egg yolks
- 325g (11½oz) whipping cream with 30% fat content

FOR THE PASTRY

- 225g (8oz) very cold slightly salted butter, cut into cubes, plus extra for greasing
- 225g (8oz) plain flour, plus extra for dusting
- ice-cold water

A good Quiche Lorraine, without cheese if you please, can be a true work of art.

- First make the pastry by crumbling the butter into the flour with your fingers or using a stand mixer. You should be aiming for a grainy texture, with enough large chunks of butter remaining to make a nice crumbly pastry.
- Add 1 or 2 tablespoons of ice-cold water, then gather the mixture together in the bowl to form a ball. Roll it out once or twice (no more) on a smooth, cold surface, then wrap the ball in clingfilm and leave in the refrigerator for 2 hours.
- Preheat the oven to 180°C (350°F), Gas Mark 4.
- Grease a cake tin, 20cm (8in) wide and 3–4cm (1¼–1½in) deep, and line the bottom with baking paper.
- Roll out the pastry on a floured surface to make a circle and use it to line the tin, leaving a little hanging over the edge. Put baking paper or foil inside the pastry case, then fill with dried or ceramic baking beans. Bake blind for 25 minutes.
- Remove from the oven, trim the edges evenly and remove the paper and beans. Set aside while you make the filling.
- Remove the rind from the pork belly, then cut the meat into fairly large pieces. Fry in a dry frying pan until cooked through, then drain on kitchen paper.
- Beat the eggs and yolks with the cream for 1 minute, until the mixture is frothy. Place half the pork belly pieces in the bottom of the pastry case and pour in the cream. Add the rest of the pork and bake for 25 minutes, keeping a careful eye on it. The top should be well risen and golden brown, and the inside should still be slightly wobbly. Slide a knife or skewer into the centre to check it is cooked through.
- Leave to cool before serving warm.

Super-cheesy quiche

SERVES 6–8
PREPARATION: 10 MINUTES
COOKING: 30–35 MINUTES

- 1 quantity shortcrust pastry (see page 41) or 1 pack ready-made
- 200g (7oz) cheese(s) crumbled and/or grated
- 250ml (9fl oz) whole milk
- 250ml (9fl oz) single cream
- 2 eggs, plus 2 egg yolks
- ¼–½ teaspoon freshly grated nutmeg
- salt and pepper

You can call this whatever you like and use whatever cheese(s) you like. Simply crumble or grate them together. Adding freshly grated nutmeg will bring out the delicate flavours even more.

- Preheat the oven to 200°C (400°F), Gas Mark 6.
- Press the pastry into a 22–24cm (8½–9½in) round baking tin and place in the refrigerator while you make the filling.
- Put the cheese(s), milk, cream, eggs and egg yolks in a mixing bowl, then whisk by hand. Season with salt and pepper and add nutmeg to taste.
- Fill the pastry case with this creamy mixture and bake for 30–35 minutes, checking after 25 minutes. If the top becomes too caramelized, cover with foil.
- Once the quiche is well risen and golden brown, remove from the oven and leave to cool for around 15 minutes before serving.

Piperade

SERVES 6–8
PREPARATION: 10 MINUTES
COOKING: 25 MINUTES

- 1–2 tablespoons olive oil
- 3 red peppers, deseeded and sliced into strips
- 2 green peppers, deseeded and sliced into strips
- 3 onions, peeled and sliced into rings
- 3 garlic cloves, peeled and finely chopped
- 5 ripe tomatoes, deseeded and chopped
- 1 bouquet garni (bay leaf, thyme, rosemary)
- pinch of Espelette or cayenne pepper
- 8–10 eggs, beaten
- 12 slices of Bayonne or Parma ham (optional)
- salt and pepper

This rustic, colourful dish is perfect for a quick and easy country lunch.

- Heat the olive oil in a large frying pan and fry the peppers with the onions and garlic, until softened (about 10 minutes).
- Add the tomatoes, bouquet garni and chilli pepper. Season lightly with salt and pepper and simmer over a low heat for 15 minutes.
- Scramble the eggs in a separate frying pan. Season and serve with the vegetables and the slices of ham, if you like.

Meadowsweet custard

SERVES 6
PREPARATION: 5 MINUTES
COOKING: 15 MINUTES
INFUSING: 1 HOUR

- 250ml (9fl oz) whole milk
- 250ml (9fl oz) double cream
- 2 heads of meadowsweet flowers (or use elderflowers or a vanilla pod)
- 5 egg yolks
- 70g (2½oz) caster sugar

Meadowsweet is a cream-coloured plant with downy flowers that appears in late summer at the same time as elderflowers. Its sweet flavours are wonderful in custard or ice cream.

- Pour the milk and cream into a saucepan, add the flowers and bring to the boil. Immediately remove from the heat and leave to infuse for 1 hour before straining and discarding the flowers.
- Beat the egg yolks in a mixing bowl with the sugar until they double in volume and turn pale.
- Bring the milk and cream mixture back to the boil, then remove from the heat. Pour over the egg mixture, stirring constantly, then put it all back in the saucepan over a medium heat.
- Stir continuously with a wooden spoon. Once the cream thickens and your finger leaves a track along the back of the spoon coated with the cream, remove from the heat and pour immediately into a bowl to halt the cooking process.
- Cool in the refrigerator before pouring into individual bowls or a large serving dish.

All about chicken

The Sunday roast chicken is practically an institution in France, a tried-and-tested formula that appeals to all meat-eaters. It also has the added bonus of smelling so good while it cooks, filling the house with a welcoming, appetizing aroma. In the French countryside, you're never far from a good poultry producer who pampers their chickens and sells them at the local market.

Roasting a chicken

...or two? If there are more than six of you, you need two chickens, in my reckoning. Unless of course you're cooking poussin, in which case you serve half a bird per person, which avoids the issue of whether people prefer the breast or leg.

Admittedly, your oven needs to be big enough, but two small chickens cooked close together in a deep-sided roasting tin should fit without any problem. That also leaves you with plenty of leftovers and carcasses that will come in handy later for soups and stocks.

There are two essential rules for cooking your chicken successfully. The first is product quality. If you don't have access to a good local producer, either through your butcher or at the market, buy the best label available at the supermarket. The second is the bird's temperature. Either cook it as soon as you get home after buying it, or take it out of the refrigerator a good 40 minutes before cooking.

The next step is to add flavour by stuffing your chicken either in the cavity or under the skin. Place it on a bed of tasty vegetables, the kind you use for making stock, then add garlic, shallots, onion, thyme, sage and/or rosemary, which will give you wonderfully tasty cooking juices. Tarragon goes particularly well with chicken. Put it in the cavity or mixed with butter under the skin, as it would burn too easily on top.

Herbes de Provence, an old favourite that is now seen as rather outdated compared to the herbs and spices from other culinary cultures, is really worth going back to, either mixed with butter under the skin, placed in the cavity, or added to the vegetables. If you do nothing else, you should at least rub the chicken all over with a halved garlic clove, massage in a little olive oil, then rub with fine salt, which you also put in the cavity. It will make all the difference.

The ideal way to cook your chicken would be to spit-roast it, basting regularly. If you haven't got a wall-mounted rotisserie, you could try the one that comes with your oven. That said, of all the ovens I have ever owned, this is the accessory that never gets unpacked! I have always followed the same recipe: preheat the oven to 220°C (425°F), Gas Mark 7, cook for 10 minutes to get things started and to dry and brown the skin, then reduce the temperature to 160–170°C (325–340°F), Gas Mark 3–4 for another 40–50 minutes, depending on the size of the chicken. I try to baste it at least once during cooking, towards the end, and I test it by gently pulling the leg away from the body and checking the colour of the meat between the leg and the rest of the carcass. If it is still pink but the skin is well browned and crisp, I cover the bird loosely with kitchen foil and cook for another 10 minutes or so.

You can also turn the chicken during cooking, which helps keep the white meat juicy, or you can heat the oil in the roasting tray and brown it on each side before putting it in the oven.

Cooking two chickens together will take longer than one, and if they are touching in the roasting tray, remember to turn them around so that all sides are well browned. Poussins require only about 45 minutes' cooking time, depending on how many you're using. And finally, if you can't find a whole bird, the quickest option is chicken pieces – choose legs or drumsticks for more flavour. They take only 40 minutes or so to cook on a bed of root vegetables, onions and garlic, plus, my personal favourite, butter and a lemon cut in wedges.

Chicken with herb butter under the skin

- Mix the herbs of your choice with 100g (3½oz) slightly salted butter. Add some pepper. Using your fingertips – be careful if you have long nails – gently lift the chicken skin either at the neck end, or (and this is easier) at the cavity end. Separate the skin from the meat on the breast and around the legs, then slide the butter into the space you have created. Close the skin and press to spread the butter out evenly. You can also spread butter on top of the chicken skin.

Stuffed roast chicken with Petit-Suisse and tarragon

- 180g (6oz) Petit-Suisse cheese (fromage frais)
- 2 shallots, peeled and finely chopped
- 3 tablespoons tarragon leaves
- 1 tablespoon olive oil
- 1 chicken, weighing about 1.5kg (3lb 5oz)
- 1 onion, peeled (optional)
- salt and pepper

A cheese from Normandy, Petit-Suisse is a badly kept 'secret' that adds succulence and flavour to the chicken. You can replace the tarragon with any fresh herbs or spices.

- Combine all the stuffing ingredients in a bowl. Mix well and use to stuff the cavity of the chicken. Close by pushing in the onion or tie with string.
- Roast the chicken as per the times on page 52.
- Tranfer the bird to a carving plate. Skim the fat from the pan and use the juices as a base for your gravy.

Chicken
with 40 garlic cloves

+ Why just 40? Use more if you like. There's no need to peel them. And don't be afraid to add onions and shallots as well. I like to cook this in a covered casserole dish, which makes the garlic more tender. If cooking a small chicken for 5 or 6 people, put it in a deep-sided cast-iron pan without a lid. Add the garlic cloves onions and so on, then add a bit of water – just 2 tablespoons – to the bottom. The garlic tastes amazing crushed on toasted croutons made just before you serve the chicken.

Chicken
with spicy seasoning

+ Just like a professional rotisserie chicken. Make a paste with olive oil, a mixture of spices of your choice and fine salt. Massage into the chicken and push the spices into the cavity as well. Place the chicken on a bed of baby potatoes in their skins and roast everything together, stirring the potatoes and basting the chicken during cooking.

Vallée d'Auge chicken

SERVES 6
PREPARATION: 5 MINUTES
COOKING: 40 MINUTES

- 2 tablespoons olive oil
- 75g (2¾oz) butter
- 3 shallots, peeled and finely chopped
- 6 chicken pieces
- 1 small glass of Calvados (optional)
- 500ml (18fl oz) dry cider
- 500g (1lb 2oz) button mushrooms, thinly sliced
- 500ml (18fl oz) single cream or crème fraîche
- 6 large firm apples, peeled, cored and quarterd
- salt and pepper

Here is a classic dish from Normandy, which combines chicken, with apples, mushrooms, cider and cream. Perfection!

- Heat the olive oil with half the butter in a heavy-based saucepan. Add the shallots and chicken pieces and brown on all sides.
- Pour in the Calvados (if using), and stir well, scraping the bottom of the pan with a wooden spatula to deglaze. If you like, you can flambé the Calvados but watch out for your eyebrows! Add the cider, scrape the bottom of the pan again to loosen the tasty caramelized bits, and bring to a gentle boil.
- In another frying pan, heat most of the remaining butter and fry the mushrooms until they release their juices. Add the mushrooms and juices to the chicken (I don't add all the juice, as I find it makes the gravy too runny, but it tastes great), season very lightly and cook for about 30 minutes.
- Add the cream and leave it to cook for another 10 minutes or so. About 5 minutes before serving, melt the remaining knob of butter in a nonstick frying pan and brown the apple quarters. Add them to the pan with the chicken, season and serve.

STAUB

Roast vegetables, gratins and cheese

It goes without saying that celeriac, cauliflower, squash and other vegetables jazzed up with herbs and spices are great meat or fish substitutes. But I'll leave that for another book. Here I'm sticking to retro comfort food cooked in the traditional French rustic style.

Cumin-roasted carrots

SERVES 6
PREPARATION: 5 MINUTES
COOKING: 30–35 MINUTES

- 8–10 large whole carrots, peeled
- 3 tablespoons olive oil
- 2–3 tablespoons cumin seeds
- 1 garlic clove, peeled and crushed
- salt and pepper

Roast vegetables are such a useful and versatile side dish – bursting with flavours, caramelized, crunchy and served hot or cold. Added to which, roasting does away with the need for any stressful last-minute steaming or boiling.

- Preheat the oven to 180°C (350°F), Gas Mark 4.
- Place the carrots in a roasting tray, add the oil and cumin seeds and toss well. Add the garlic, then season with salt and pepper.
- Roast for 30–35 minutes.

Cherry tomatoes slow-roasted in balsamic vinegar and honey

SERVES 6
PREPARATION: 10 MINUTES
COOKING: 2–2¼ HOURS

- 750g (1lb 10oz) cherry or small tomatoes
- 6 garlic cloves, peeled
- 3 tablespoons olive oil
- 1 tablespoon runny honey
- 3 tablespoons balsamic vinegar
- salt and pepper

- Preheat the oven to 150°C (300°F), Gas Mark 2.
- Slice the tomatoes in half and place them in a gratin dish (cut-side down) with the garlic cloves. Mix the oil, honey and vinegar, then pour over the tomatoes.
- Bake for 2–2¼ hours until the tomatoes are caramelized.

Provençal vegetable tian

SERVES 6
PREPARATION: 20 MINUTES
COOKING: 40 MINUTES

- 1 garlic clove, peeled and halved
- 5 tomatoes, washed and cut into 5mm (¼in) slices
- 2 courgettes, washed and cut into 5mm (¼in) slices
- 2 aubergines, washed and cut into 5mm (¼in) slices
- 1 onion, peeled and cut into 5mm (¼in) slices
- 2 sprigs of thyme
- 2 sprigs of rosemary
- 2 bay leaves, torn in half
- olive oil, for drizzling
- salt and pepper
- fresh basil, to garnish

It takes a bit of teamwork to get the presentation of this dish right, but it's well worth the effort. You can also add a layer of chopped tomatoes under the other vegetables for more moistness and flavour.

- Preheat the oven to 180°C (350°F), Gas Mark 4. Rub the inside of a large baking dish (in France you can actually get a special tian dish) with the garlic clove, then slice it finely.
- Arrange the vegetable slices in the dish as upright as possible, alternating the colours and popping a slice of garlic in every now and then. Slot the thyme, rosemary and bay leaves in between the vegetable slices and make sure they are tightly packed.
- Drizzle over olive oil and season with salt and pepper.
- Bake for around 40 minutes (less if you're making several tians in smaller dishes).
- Remove from the oven when the edges of the vegetables are well-browned, and serve hot or warm, garnished with a little fresh basil.

Caramelized butternut squash gratin
with melted cheese

SERVES 6
PREPARATION: 10 MINUTES
COOKING: 45–50 MINUTES

- 1 butternut squash, washed, deseeded and sliced lengthways
- 3–4 garlic cloves, peeled and crushed
- 3 tablespoons olive oil
- 300g (10½oz) Camembert, Brie or Reblochon cheese
- salt and pepper
- fresh thyme leaves, to garnish

And it's as easy as that. Everything about this recipe is all in the name, which combines three of my favourite words: caramelized, gratin and cheese.

- Preheat the oven to 180°C (350°F), Gas Mark 4.
- Rub garlic on the butternut slices, then massage in the oil. Season with salt and pepper and roast for around 40 minutes. The butternut slices should be caramelized and tender but still firm.
- Slice the cheese and place on top of the butternut. Put back in the oven for 5–10 minutes, until you have a bubbly gratin. Garnish with thyme leaves and serve immediately.

Potato gratin with Coulommiers cheese

SERVES 6–8
PREPARATION: 20 MINUTES
COOKING: 40 MINUTES

- 2kg (4lb 8oz) potatoes (Bintje, Anya or similar)
- 1 garlic clove, peeled and halved
- 1 very ripe Coulommiers cheese
- ½ teaspoon freshly grated or ground nutmeg
- 300ml (10fl oz) single cream
- salt and pepper
- fresh thyme leaves, to garnish

I've chosen Coulommiers cheese simply because it's larger than the more commonly used Camembert. This is a side dish to accompany simple roast meat, chicken, or grilled fish rather than a stew or a dish with sauce, such as a blanquette or bourguignon. It could even become a main dish with the addition of bacon lardons and melt-in-the mouth onions, as in a tartiflette.

- Preheat the oven to 160°C (325°F), Gas Mark 3.
- Peel and slice the potatoes as thinly as possible, using a mandoline if necessary.
- Rub the inside of your gratin dish with the garlic clove.
- Either slice the cheese horizontally, keeping half of it to put on top, or leave it whole if you prefer. Alternate the slices of potato with the slices of cheese. Add the nutmeg to the cream and season lightly with salt and pepper. Pour the cream on top and let it soak into the potatoes.
- Layer the remaining half of the cheese on the gratin and bake for about 40 minutes. You want the top to be golden brown and the cheese lovely and melty. Garnish with a few thyme leaves and serve piping hot.

Pear and blue cheese puff pastry tarts

SERVES 6
PREPARATION: 15 MINUTES
COOKING: 20–25 MINUTES

- 6 squares of ready-made puff pastry (about 20cm/8in in size)
- 1 egg, beaten
- 3 ripe but firm pears
- 3 tablespoons mascarpone cheese
- 200g (7oz) blue cheese
- fresh thyme leaves, to garnish (optional)

A great compromise between cheese and dessert, or perfect as a delicious autumnal starter.

- Preheat the oven to 200°C (400°F), Gas Mark 6.
- Place the pastry squares on a baking tray and score them with a knife 2cm (¾in) from the edges to make a frame, taking care not to cut all the way through the pastry. That way the edges will rise more than the inside to frame the cheese and pears.
- Brush the edges of the squares with beaten egg, so that they brown when cooked.
- Peel the pears and cut in half lengthways. Place each half flat side down, then slice from top to bottom, keeping the stalk end joined. Press lightly on each half to spread them into a fan shape.
- Spread a little mascarpone in the middle of the squares and place the fanned pear halves on top. Crumble the blue cheese over them and bake for 20–25 minutes.
- Once the cheese has fully melted and begun to caramelize, and the edges of the pastry squares have risen and turned golden brown, remove from the oven and serve immediately, garnished with a few thyme leaves, if you like.

Dauphiné ravioli gratin with leeks and Comté cheese

SERVES 6
PREPARATION: 10 MINUTES
COOKING: 20 MINUTES

- 50g (1¾oz) butter
- 1 large leek, washed and sliced into rounds
- 1kg (2lb 4oz) ready-made Dauphiné ravioli, separated (see recipe intro)
- 200–250ml (7–9fl oz) single cream
- 100g (3½oz) Comté cheese, grated
- salt and pepper

Originally from the Dauphiné region in southwest France, bordering Italy, this gratin is great comfort food but is often overlooked. It uses shop-bought small ravioli filled with Comté and Gruyère cheese, but if you can't find these, buy the smallest mild cheese ravioli available. This is wonderful served with grilled or roast meat, or even on its own for a veggie meal.

- Preheat the oven to 180°C (350°F), Gas Mark 4.
- Heat the butter in a large frying pan and cook the leek over a low heat. You want it to be tender but not over-browned.
- Cook the ravioli in boiling water according to the packet instructions, then drain.
- Mix the leeks into the ravioli, season and tip everything into a large gratin dish. Pour over the cream until completely covered, then sprinkle with the grated cheese.
- Bake in the oven for about 15 minutes, keeping an eye on it. You want the top to be nicely browned. Remove from the oven and serve piping hot.

Artichokes with blue cheese sauce

SERVES 6
PREPARATION: 5 MINUTES
COOKING: 45 MINUTES

- 6 large artichokes, rinsed
- 350g (12oz) blue cheese
- 500ml (18fl oz) single cream

My favourite way to eat artichokes.

- Cook the artichokes in a large saucepan of boiling water or in a pressure cooker.
- Check whether they are cooked by pulling a leaf at the base of the artichoke – it shoud come off easily.
- Melt the blue cheese into the cream and spoon the sauce into small bowls for your guests to dip the leaves in as they eat.

Mustard sauce

SERVES 6–8
PREPARATION: 2 MINUTES

- 400ml (14fl oz) crème fraîche
- 2 tablespoons strong mustard
- 1 tablespoon wholegrain mustard
- salt and pepper

- Mix the crème fraîche with both types of mustard. Season and serve in small bowls alongside the artichokes, then eat as above.

Serving cheese

When it comes to French-style country lunches, cheese is your best friend. A loyal companion who doesn't mind whether he's the guest of honour, just another guest, a last-minute fill-in or even not invited at all. He won't be offended and will always be there when you need him, either to make up the numbers or as the centrepiece. He can be part of any conversation, adapted to all your guests' tastes and styles, arrives ready to go, looks good, is easy to handle, has his own vocabulary, and is liked and understood by everyone.

A few years ago, while living with a vegan, cheese was banned from my French kitchen – an ordeal I wouldn't wish on my worst enemy. I think I am still over-compensating for that trauma and is probably why cheese is such a big part of my menus for friends and family today. Even though it is a hassle to have to change the plates and cutlery and remember to serve the salad (if I'm having one), cheese is always at the top of my shopping list. When I plan my menus, it automatically gets pride of place without having to elbow its way in or beg to be included.

In summer, I love to put together a 100% fresh, 100% goats' cheese platter. With plenty of red fruit available, it's the easiest season to serve cheese and dessert together, or even completely blur the boundaries by plating a lovely large, well-matured Corsican Brousse with honey and strawberries or cherries. In late autumn, it is such a joy to bring out a plate of just one magnificent mature blue cheese in all its solitary glory, accompanied by apples and pears at peak perfection.

And with any variety that is matured to a tee, it is perfectly acceptable in France to serve it on its own so you can enjoy it to the full. Just accessorize it carefully: a good fruit loaf, fig jam, or cider or wine jelly will complement the flavour.

Putting together a big, beautiful, old-fashioned cheese board is an art in itself. If you are lucky enough to be able to buy from a cheesemonger, or even directly from a producer, and they have time to advise you, it is such a treat and a great way to learn, too. The rules are quite flexible but they usually suggest five types of cheese as the optimum number: a blue (with its own knife for no cross contamination of flavour), a hard cheese, such as an aged Salers, a light, fresh goats' or sheep's milk cheese, a good ripe and runny Camembert or Saint-Félicien, plus one other: either your cheesemonger's current recommendation, or one you just can't resist.

Be generous and bear in mind when you're choosing that you'll probably have leftovers to use for most of the following week. And during your lunch, if appetites dip, or it's a lovely day and you want to go for a walk or swim rather than lingering around the table, so you end up not serving your lovely selection, there's a whole world of recipe possibilities out there for your uneaten treasures.

Roasted fruit
for cheese and dessert

SERVES 6
PREPARATION: 5 MINUTES
COOKING: 20 MINUTES

- about 1kg (2lb 4oz) of your chosen fruit
- 2 tablespoons runny honey
- a few sprigs of rosemary and/or thyme (optional)

FIGS AND/OR GRAPES

Sun-kissed juicy figs and grapes taste even more wonderful after being popped in a hot oven for a while. I like to serve them with a goats' cheese platter in summer and autumn, or with one of the cakes from my little collection (see pages 92–101).

- Preheat the oven to 180°C (350°F), Gas Mark 4.
- Place the fruits in an ovenproof dish.
- Add a little honey, rosemary or thyme, if you like, and roast until they release their juices for maximum flavour.

SERVES 6
PREPARATION: 5 MINUTES
COOKING: 20 MINUTES

- 6 fairly ripe peaches, rinsed
- 2 tablespoons runny honey
- juice of 2 oranges
- a few sprigs of thyme

PEACHES

- Preheat the oven to 180°C (350°F), Gas Mark 4.
- Put the peaches in a small ovenproof dish with the honey, orange juice and thyme. Cover the dish and bake for 20 minutes.
- Leave to cool before serving in the cooking juices.

Fig, walnut and hazelnut jam

MAKES 6 JARS
PREPARATION: 15 MINUTES
COOKING: 1 HOUR

- 2kg (4lb 8oz) very ripe purple figs, ideally picked straight from the tree
- 2 large handfuls of walnut kernels
- 1 large handful of shelled hazelnuts
- about 1.5kg (3lb 5oz) caster sugar

When he came round for lunch one day, my friend Pascal brought me a jar of his homemade jam, which tasted incredible and goes perfectly with cheese. Then he generously shared his precious recipe with me. Thank you, Pascal!

- Wash the figs thoroughly, dry them and cut into quarters (or 6 pieces if they are very big).
- Crush the walnuts and hazelnuts into small pieces.
- Tip the figs and nuts into a large flameproof casserole dish and cook over a low heat for about 45 minutes, stirring frequently. Remove from the heat.
- Weigh the cooked fruit and nuts and add 750g (1lb 10oz) sugar per kilo (2lb 4oz) (adding less sugar means that it might not keep as well).
- Put back over a very high heat for 15 minutes, stirring constantly.
- Fill 6 sterilized jars (see Tip) as full as you can, put the lids on and turn them upside down to expel the air and make sure they seal properly.

TIP

To sterilize jam jars (and their lids), wash in hot soapy water, rinse well and place upside down on a baking tray. Place in a preheated oven at 120°C (275°F), Gas Mark 1, for 20 minutes.

Quick fruit compote with fresh herbs

SERVES 4–6
PREPARATION: 5 MINUTES
COOLING: 30 MINUTES

- 300g (10½oz) fresh raspberries, rinsed and drained
- 1 sprig of fresh rosemary or fresh thyme, or both
- 2 teaspoons granulated sugar (optional)

The fresh, sharp fruit and summer herb flavours are terrific with new season goats' cheeses or a soft, rich Brillat-Savarin. You can use stoned amd chopped ripe plums, damsons or cherries, and play around with herbs in season. Tarragon, bay, woodruff and oregano all work well.

- Put the fruit and the sugar, if using, into a small pan with a dash of water. Cook over medium heat for 2–3 minutes. The fruit will release its juices as it cooks.
- Add the herbs, and stir the into the fruit. Let the compote bubble for just a minute or so, leaving some pieces of raspberry for texture.
- Remove from the heat and leave to cool with the herbs, so as their flavour infuses. Once cooled, remove the herbs. Serve cold or slightly warm.

Cakes

Here is a small collection of essential French cake recipes with seasonal variations that can easily be served with different kinds of raw or puréed fruit. They are also perfect to take with you as a dessert when visiting friends or family. They are great to accompany afternoon tea, too. Make enough to be able to offer some for your guests to take home with them.

Le Comptoir du Porche

George Sand's chocolate cake

SERVES 6–8
PREPARATION: 10-15 MINUTES
COOKING: 35 MINUTES

- 250g (9oz) good-quality dark chocolate (at least 70% cocoa solids)
- 100g (3½oz) unsalted butter, plus extra for greasing
- 4 eggs, separated
- 100g (3½oz) caster sugar
- 100g (3½oz) ground almonds
- ½ teaspoon vanilla extract
- pinch of salt

One of my favourite heroines of all time, George (Aurore) Sand, loved to entertain and excelled at playing the host. Here is her famous cake, perfect with fresh or puréed fruit, or a vanilla custard. Always better the day after it's made.

- Preheat the oven to 180°C (350°F), Gas Mark 4. Grease a 22cm (8½in) cake tin.
- Very gently, melt the chocolate with the butter in a bain-marie (a heatproof bowl set over a pan of simmering water) or in a microwave, stirring frequently.
- Make sure the mixture is not too hot, then add the egg yolks one by one, breaking them with the back of a wooden spoon before stirring them in.
- Set aside 2 tablespoons of sugar. Add the rest, along with the ground almonds, to the chocolate mixture and stir again.
- Whisk the egg whites with the remaining sugar. Delicately fold them into the chocolate mixture, lifting it up to keep in as much air as possible.
- Pour the mixture into the greased cake tin and bake for 35 minutes. Leave to stand for 10 minutes before turning it out.

Petit Baulois chocolate fondant cake

SERVES 6–8
PREPARATION: 5 MINUTES
COOKING: 40-45 MINUTES
STANDING: 5–6 HOURS

- 150g (5½oz) light brown sugar
- 5 eggs
- 200g (7oz) good-quality dark chocolate (at least 70% cocoa solids)
- 200g (7oz) slightly salted butter, plus extra for greasing
- 1 heaped tablespoon salted butter caramel spread
- 1 tablespoon plain flour

Originally from La Baule, in Brittany, this rich, sweet cake with a crunchy, almost meringue-like crust is known as a gâteau de voyage in France, meaning that it keeps well enough to take on long journeys. One of France's most popular cakes, this recipe is my attempt to replicate something of its texture and caramel flavours, but of course nothing could replace the original.

- Preheat the oven to 210°C (415°F), Gas Mark 6–7. Grease a 20cm (8in) springform cake tin. If you don't have one, line a shallow cake tin with baking paper for easier removal.
- In a mixer bowl, whisk the sugar with the eggs until the mixture turns pale and frothy and doubles in volume.
- Very gently melt the chocolate with the butter in a bain-marie (a heatproof bowl set over a pan of simmering water) or in a microwave, stirring frequently. Heat the caramel briefly over a low heat to make it runnier, then stir into the melted chocolate. Pour this into the mixer bowl containing the eggs, beating gently to blend everything together.
- Finally, add the flour and mix one last time.
- Pour the mixture into the cake tin and bake for 5 minutes. Reduce the oven temperature to 120°C (250°F), Gas Mark ½ and continue baking for 30–35 minutes. The centre of the cake should stay wobbly to achieve the famous texture.
- Remove from the oven and leave the cake to cool and stand for at least 5–6 hours before serving. Release or lift out the tin and transfer to a pretty plate. Remember, this is the ultimate gift cake – it's not called gâteau de voyage for nothing!

Lemon cake

SERVES 8
PREPARATION: 10 MINUTES
COOKING: 40 MINUTES
STANDING: 15 MINUTES

- 50g (1¾oz) slightly salted butter, at room temperature, plus extra for greasing
- 150g (5½oz) caster sugar, plus 1 tablespoon
- 150g (5½oz) plain flour, plus extra for dusting
- 2 teaspoons baking powder
- juice and grated zest of 1 lemon
- 2 eggs
- 125ml (4fl oz) whole milk

Great with a citrus fruit salad for a winter lunch.

- Preheat the oven to 170°C (340°F), Gas Mark 3–4. Butter and flour a 22cm (8½in) loaf tin.
- Using an electric whisk or a stand mixer, whisk the butter and 150g (5½oz) sugar together until the mixture turns pale and frothy. Fold in the flour, baking powder and lemon zest.
- Beat the eggs and milk together, then stir into the flour mixture. Pour into the prepared tin, then bake for about 40 minutes. Check while cooking that the cake is not browning too much. Slide a skewer into the middle and if it comes out clean, the cake is done.
- Remove from the oven, mix the lemon juice and tablespoon of sugar together and pour over the cake so that it soaks in. Leave to cool and absorb the juice in the tin but be careful not to let the sugar dry completely before turning the cake out, otherwise it will stick.

Savoy cake

SERVES 6–8
PREPARATION: 10 MINUTES
COOKING: 40–45 MINUTES

- knob of butter, for greasing
- 6 eggs, separated
- 200g (7oz) caster sugar
- 75g (2¾oz) plain flour
- 75g (2¾oz) cornflour
- grated zest of 1 lemon
- icing sugar, to serve

Suitable for any occasion, this super-light sponge cake is excellent all year round with fresh or puréed fruit. Find a nice decorative cake mould and fill the centre of the cake with fruit before serving.

- Preheat the oven to 180°C (350°F), Gas Mark 4. Butter a 24cm (9½in) ring cake tin.
- In the bowl of your stand mixer (or using an electric whisk), whisk the egg yolks with the sugar until the mixture doubles in volume and turns pale.
- Using a spatula, gently fold in the flour, cornflour and lemon zest.
- Whisk the egg whites into stiff peaks and fold them into the cake mixture.
- Pour the mixture into the prepared tin, smoothing over the surface. Bake for 40–45 minutes, checking whether it is cooked by sliding a skewer into one of the deepest parts of the cake. If it comes out clean, it's done. Leave to cool slightly before turning out.
- Dust with icing sugar just before serving.

Hazelnut cake

SERVES 6–8
PREPARATION: 15 MINUTES
COOKING: 25–30 MINUTES

- 5 egg whites
- 80g (2¾oz) ground hazelnuts
- 150g (5½oz) caster sugar
- 75g (2¾oz) plain flour
- 100g (3½oz) slightly salted melted butter, plus extra for greasing
- icing sugar, to serve

Out of all the sponge cakes, this is probably my favourite. The flavour of the hazelnuts comes through beautifully and goes perfectly with the butter. The texture particularly suits puréed autumn fruit (figs, plums, apples).

- Preheat the oven to 200°C (400°F), Gas Mark 6. Grease a 22cm (8½in) cake tin.
- Beat the egg whites until stiff. Add the hazelnuts and sugar, then fold in carefully, lifting the mixture to keep in as much air as possible. Repeat with the flour and finally the melted butter.
- Pour the mixture into the prepared tin and bake for 15 minutes. Reduce the temperature to 150°C (300F), Gas Mark 2 and bake for a further 10–15 minutes.
- Check while cooking to make sure the cake is not too brown on top. If it is, cover with foil. To test if the cake is ready, slide a skewer into the middle – if it comes out clean, it's done!
- Remove from the oven and cool slightly before turning it out on a wire rack. Dust the cake with icing sugar just before serving.

Fruit tarts

The idea that you are never more than 30 minutes away from a delicious seasonal fruit tart makes me so happy. Along with roast chicken and strong cheeses, it is an integral part of French country cooking.

Whether or not you choose to make your fruit tart from scratch, you have several options. You can use ready-made pastry and frozen fruit (only if you're really desperate and time is against you) or you can use homemade pastry and fruit picked from the garden. I usually go for something in between, with a good-quality ready-made shortcrust pastry and seasonal fruit from the market. And I never make my own puff pastry. However, here are some recipes for homemade pastry and crumble that will make all the difference to your bakes. You just need to have a little time to spare, not only to make them but also to allow them to chill. Remember to keep a good vanilla ice cream in the freezer, and/or yogurt or crème fraîche in the refrigerator and you will always be ready to serve.

Buckwheat flour and olive oil pastry

SERVES 6–8
PREPARATION: 5 MINUTES
CHILLING: 30 MINUTES

- 300g (10½oz) plain flour
- 50g (1¾oz) buckwheat flour
- ½ teaspoon salt
- 2 tablespoons light brown sugar
- 150ml (5fl oz) olive oil
- 4–5 tablespoons ice-cold water

Buckwheat is a gluten-free grain and produces a slightly more rustic pastry than regular wheat. This pastry is also dairy-free.

- Put both flours into a large mixing bowl, add the salt and sugar and mix well. Pour in the oil in a thin stream, mixing with a knife to distribute it evenly. You should end up with a grainy mixture.
- Mix in the ice-cold water a spoonful at a time until a dough forms that you can gather into a ball. It will be slightly stickier than a butter-based pastry. Cover in clingfilm and leave to rest in the freezer for 30 minutes before using.

Classic sweet shortcrust pastry

SERVES 6–8
PREPARATION: 5 MINUTES
CHILLING: 2 HOURS

- 250g (9oz) plain flour
- 2 tablespoons caster sugar
- 125g (4½oz) very cold slightly salted butter, cut into small pieces
- 3–4 tablespoons very cold water

- Prepare the pastry a few hours before you need to use it. Mix the flour and sugar together in a bowl, then rub in the butter with your fingertips until you get a grainy texture.
- Mix in the water a spoonful at a time until a dough forms that you can gather into a ball.
- Cover in clingfilm and leave to rest in the refrigerator for at least 2 hours.

Richer shortcrust pastry

SERVES 6–8
PREPARATION: 10 MINUTES
CHILLING: 2 HOURS

- 250g (9oz) plain flour, plus extra for dusting
- 150g (5½oz) very cold slightly salted butter
- 75g (2¾oz) icing sugar
- 60g (2¼oz) ground almonds
- ½ teaspoon vanilla extract
- 1 egg, beaten

- Place all the ingredients except the vanilla and egg in your stand mixer bowl and blend until the mixture resembles coarse sand. This takes around 30 seconds.
- Add the vanilla and egg and mix again.
- When the pastry starts to stick to the beaters, switch off the mixer and remove the pastry. Place it on a cold lightly floured surface and form into a ball.
- Wrap in clingfilm and leave to rest in the refrigerator for 2 hours.

Classic crumble mix

SERVES 6–8
PREPARATION: 5 MINUTES

- 150g (5½oz) plain flour
- 60g (2¼oz) rolled oats
- 100g (3½oz) light brown or demerara sugar
- 150g (5½oz) slightly salted butter

I know this is not traditionally French, but 'le crumbeul' has become so widely adopted in France that it would be wrong not to include it in this section. Crumble takes slightly longer to cook than a tart, but requires a lot less work.

- Put all the ingredients into your mixer bowl and blend until quite grainy, leaving some larger pieces. (This can be done by hand if you prefer.)
- The crumble can be used straight away, sprinkled over apples or any other acidic fruit mixture.

Frangipane

- 125g (4½oz) slightly salted butter, softened
- 2 eggs
- 125g (4½oz) caster sugar
- 180g (6oz) ground almonds
- a few drops of almond extract (optional)

I love this baked with apricots and figs, and served warm.

- Place the butter, eggs and sugar in your mixer bowl and beat until smooth.
- Add the ground almonds, the almond extract, if you like, and mix well.
- Store in the refrigerator for up to 7 days, until you want to use it – perhaps in the fig tart on page 115.

Samaritaine

Tarte Tatin

SERVES 6
PREPARATION: 20 MINUTES
COOKING: 25 MINUTES

- 3 or 4 large acidic apples (Granny Smith or Bramley)
- 100g (3½oz) caster sugar
- 2 tablespoons water
- 75g (2¾oz) slightly salted butter
- 1 pack ready-made puff pastry
- plain flour, for dusting

TO SERVE (OPTIONAL)

- 2–3 tablespoons caster sugar
- dash of Calvados or Pommeau
- 200g (7oz) crème fraîche

A Tarte Tatin is marvellous when you get it right. Everyone loves it, and it is so easy to make once you know how.

- Preheat the oven to 180°C (350°F), Gas Mark 4.
- Peel, halve and core the apples. Heat the sugar and water in a small, ovenproof frying pan, ideally a 20cm (8in) one in which you can bake the tart too. Otherwise, simply use a heavy-based frying pan of any size. Once a syrup has formed, let it bubble away, shaking the pan so that the mixture caramelizes evenly (don't stir with a spoon, as this may cause the sugar to crystallize).
- When the caramel is a lovely golden colour (1–2 minutes), take it off the heat and add the butter – carefully in case it spits! Stir gently with a wooden spoon until smooth. Add the apple halves and cook gently over a low heat for 3–4 minutes.
- Arrange the apples cut-side up in the small pan, or transfer to a similar-sized cake tin and pour the caramel over them.
- Roll out the pastry on a lightly floured surface and use to cover the apples, tucking it in all around the edge, like a bed sheet. However, if you are planning to bake the tart later, allow the apples to cool before placing the pastry on top, then set aside in a cool place (not the refrigerator, as this will be too cold) until you are ready to bake it.
- Bake for about 25 minutes, until the pastry is golden brown. When ready, let it rest for about 5 minutes before inverting it into a deep plate that will hold the caramel and cooking juices too.
- Mix the 2–3 tablespoons of sugar with the Calvados or Pommeau, stir in the crème fraîche and serve with the hot tart if you wish.

TIP
Tarte Tatin is equally delicious served with plain crème fraîche or vanilla ice cream.

Pear and chocolate amandine tart

SERVES 6–8
PREPARATION: 20 MINUTES
COOKING: 40 MINUTES

- 1 quantity sweet shortcrust pastry (see page 105) or 1 pack ready-made
- 50g (1¾oz) ground almonds, plus extra for dusting
- 200ml (7fl oz) single cream
- 180g (6oz) good-quality dark chocolate (at least 70% cocoa solids), chopped
- 1 egg
- 2 heaped tablespoons crème fraîche
- 80g (2¾oz) caster sugar
- 12 canned pear halves

TO SERVE (OPTIONAL)

- a few chopped almonds
- icing sugar

A superb dessert for special occasions with a great combination of textures. The trick is to prevent the moist ingredients – the chocolate ganache and the pears – from making the pastry or almond sponge wet.

- Preheat the oven to 180°C (350°F), Gas Mark 4.
- Using your fingers, press and stretch the pastry into the bottom of a 22–24cm (8½–9½in) springform cake tin. Place baking paper and ceramic baking beans (or lentils, rice, etc.) on top of the pastry. Bake blind for 10–15 minutes, until the edges are lightly browned. Set aside to cool.
- Dust the cooled pastry with ground almonds (this will stop the chocolate from making it soggy) and place in the refrigerator.
- To make the chocolate ganache, bring the cream to the boil in a saucepan, then remove from the heat and add the chocolate. Let it melt for a few moments, then stir into the cream until the mixture turns shiny. Allow to cool for a few minutes, then pour it onto the tart base and return immediately to the refrigerator.
- To make the almond sponge, beat the egg, crème fraîche, measured ground almonds and sugar together in a bowl by hand or with an electric whisk, to form a thick paste.
- Increase the oven temperature to 190°C (375°F), Gas Mark 5. Cut 6 of the pear halves into small pieces. Spread them over the cold chocolate base.
- Arrange the remaining halves on top, pointed ends towards the middle. Pour the almond sponge mixture over them.
- Bake for around 30 minutes in the lower part of the oven to make sure that the pastry base cooks through.

- When the top and edges of the pastry are golden brown, remove the tart from the oven and leave it to cool before putting it in the refrigerator. The tart is best eaten later the same day, or even the day after, as the chocolate will harden and all the flavours will blend together.
- If you wish, sprinkle over some chopped almonds and dust with icing sugar just before serving.

Fig tart with frangipane

SERVES 6–8
PREPARATION: 10 MINUTES
COOKING: 30–35 MINUTES

- 1 pack ready-made shortcrust pastry
- 300g (10½oz) frangipane (see page 107)
- 6–8 fresh figs, washed, dried and halved

- Preheat the oven to 180°C (350°F), Gas Mark 4.
- Using your fingers, press and stretch the pastry into the bottom of a 24cm (9½in) springform cake tin. Spread with the frangipane and place the halved figs on top (skin-side down).
- Bake for 30–35 minutes, until the top is golden brown and puffy.
- Remove from the oven and leave to cool slightly before serving.

Christmas menu

You've taken out your best table linen, laid out your plates, cutlery and napkins beautifully, lit dozens of candles and fetched your best bottles from your wine collection, where they have been patiently awaiting the festivities. The menu offered in the following pages boasts all kinds of rich, luxurious ingredients, but these traditional Christmas dishes are still fairly simple to make and present.

Roast goose with apples

Cooking a goose for Christmas always seemed like a bit too much fuss to me. First, it's a struggle to find a good-quality bird from a trusted producer, and then there's all that fat produced during roasting. But it turned out that my friendly firewood delivery man is also a poultry breeder, and he kindly delivered one of his fine birds to be cooked for this book, and now I am hooked.

Once again, my friends, it is a shame that you can't taste the flavours through the pages. Goose meat is dark and rich – fatty, admittedly, but absolutely scrumptious, with a slight gamey flavour. It takes a good part of the day to cook, but is well worth the effort.

Goose is a bit like duck in that its carcass seems disproportionately large for the amount of meat it gives – far less than a standard chicken. For six people, you'll need the smallest size (4.5–5kg/ 9lb 13oz–11lb), and for eight to ten people, go for a 6kg (13lb) goose. Allow 30 minutes' cooking time per 1kg (2lb 4oz) of non-stuffed meat, but this is not an exact science, so you should always check the bird regularly during cooking or, at the very least, 30 minutes before the end of cooking.

You can reduce the amount of fat rendered during cooking by removing the reserves in the cavity. Collect it all in a jar and keep it to roast the potatoes for the meal, and for other times when you fancy a treat.

SERVES 8–10
PREPARATION: 20 MINUTES
COOKING: ABOUT 3 HOURS
STANDING: 20 MINUTES

FOR THE BIRD

- 1 goose weighing 6kg (13lb)
- 2 onions, peeled
- salt

FOR THE APPLES

- around 12 acidic apples (ideally Granny Smith or Bramley)
- 400g (14oz) dried fruit and nut mixture (cranberries, raisins, pecanss, walnuts, etc.)
- salt and pepper

- Preheat the oven to 220°C (425°F), Gas Mark 7. Rub salt into the goose and prick the skin in places to help the fat drain out.
- Place the onions in the goose cavity. Wrap the wings in foil to protect them. Put the goose on a rack in a fairly deep roasting tin and roast for 45 minutes.
- Drain the fat from the tin and reduce the oven temperature to 150°C (300°F), Gas Mark 2. Cook for a further 2–2½ hours. As the meat is already dark, check the colour of the cooking juice that runs out when you cut into the base of a leg. It needs to be light in colour but not pink or red, which would indicate blood. If the skin is starting to burn, cover the top with foil to continue cooking. But remember, the skin should be crisp!
- When there is slightly less than an hour of cooking time left, prepare the fruit, which will cook with the goose. Core the apples and stuff the hollow with the dried fruit mixture. Place them in a roasting dish.
- Around 40 minutes before the goose is cooked, baste the apples with a little goose fat and season with salt and pepper. Bake in the oven until they are tender and slightly split.
- Once the goose is cooked, remove it from the oven, cover with foil and leave to stand for 20 minutes before carving and serving. If the apples are not cooked enough, leave them in the oven while the goose is resting.

Winter vegetables in chicken stock

SERVES 8–10
COOKING: 30–35 MINUTES

- 2 leeks, white parts only
- 2 onions
- 10 firm potatoes
- 4–5 small turnips
- 3 carrots
- 3 parsnips
- 2 litres (3½ pints) good-quality chicken stock
- 1 bouquet garni (bay leaf, thyme, rosemary)
- salt and pepper

- Peel all the vegetables and chop them into 2–3cm (¾–1¼in) pieces.
- Bring the stock to the boil and poach all the vegetables and the bouquet garni for around 30 minutes, or less if you prefer them crunchy.
- Once they are cooked, remove from the stock, keep them warm and reduce the cooking liquid for 5 minutes so that it just coats the vegetables. Season before serving.

TIP

A little grated truffle on top would not go amiss at this point.

Scallop, langoustine and foie gras vol-au-vents

I have followed the same basic principles for 20 years and it's made my life so much easier. Why exhaust yourself trying to make complicated things when the professionals do a much better job? All that wasted time and energy could be redirected to activities (or recipes!) that would give you a lot more pleasure and a real sense of achievement. So I generally buy puff pastry from my local bakery, but sometimes buy frozen. For me, ordering for a special occasion from my favourite shops, and then going to collect the goodies, is part of the fun of planning a meal. Nothing feels more special, or ultimately more human, than being part of a crowd at a market with other food lovers, knowing that we are all experiencing the same sensations and emotions.

I never compromise when it comes to the freshness of the ingredients for this filling, which spills deliciously out of the vol-au-vents. This is a straightforward recipe that can mostly be made and cooked the same day as your lunch, and the creamy sauce can happily be made in the morning and gently reheated 10 minutes or so before serving.

The foie gras isn't compulsory, but personally I love that decadent surf and turf feel. If you decide to use it, cook it shortly before serving (ideally while you are reheating the seafood sauce) so that its crisp exterior provides a lovely contrast in texture. I cook my foie gras escalopes straight out of the freezer, as they hold their shape better when cooked from frozen.

I always make (very) generous portions and allow for extra filling, so feel free to reduce the quantity (including the size of the vol-au-vent cases) for a less copious starter.

SERVES 8–10
PREPARATION: 25 MINUTES
COOKING: 20 MINUTES

- 24–30 cleaned scallops (with or without roe, according to preference)
- 50g (1¾oz) butter, cut into cubes
- 24 –30 large raw langoustines
- 8–10 vol-au-vent cases from the bakery, or frozen
- 250g (9oz) raw foie gras escalopes (slices about 2cm/¾in thick, optional)
- salt and pepper

FOR THE CHAMPAGNE SAUCE

- 200g (7oz) shallots, peeled and finely chopped
- small knob of butter
- 100ml (3½fl oz) lemon juice
- 400–500ml (14–18fl oz) champagne
- 500g (1lb 2oz) very cold butter, cut into cubes
- 750ml (27fl oz) double cream

- When it comes to cooking scallops, I confess to a slight preference for using the oven, which gives a more evenly cooked result. But you can pan-fry them too, of course.
- Preheat the oven to 180°C (350°F), Gas Mark 4. Place the scallops on a baking tray and dot the cubes of butter on top. Season very lightly with salt and pepper. Roast for 5 minutes: the scallops should be very lightly browned, but still pearly white inside. Remove them from the oven, cover in foil and set aside in a cool spot in the kitchen, avoiding the refrigerator if possible.
- For the langoustines, bring a large pan of salted water to the boil. Drop them in and cook for 2 minutes and no more, the time it takes for the water to come to the boil again and the langoustines to rise to the surface. Drain, set aside 6–8 to use as garnish, and leave the rest to cool before peeling them to remove the tails. Set the peeled langoustines aside in a cool place, again avoiding the refrigerator, if possible.
- Prepare the sauce: sweat the shallots in a large frying pan with the butter, without browning. Deglaze the pan with the lemon juice and stir well. Pour in the champagne and bring to the boil. Simmer for a few minutes to reduce by a half, then,gradually add the butter, whisking to emulsify. Pour in the cream to stabilize the sauce and season with salt and pepper. Keep warm.

- About 15 minutes before serving, just as your guests are finishing their glasses of champagne and starting to take their seats, assemble the vol-au-vents. Heat them on a baking tray in the oven at 150°C (300°F), Gas Mark 2 (still warm after cooking the goose). Meanwhile, drop the scallops and the langoustines into the sauce and reheat very gently, carefully stirring from time to time.
- If using foie gras, line a plate with kitchen paper, then heat a dry non-stick frying pan until very hot. Pan-fry the escalopes for 1 minute on each side, until the surface is golden brown and crisp. Warning – this may produce a lot of smoke! Drain the escalopes on a paper-lined plate, then cut into pieces about 2cm (¾in) and add to the saucepan with the rest of the filling.
- Place the vol-au-vents on a serving dish, keeping the pastry lids to one side. Spoon in the filling and sauce, garnish with the whole langoustines that were set aside and pop a pastry lid on top of each vol-au-vent. Serve the remaining filling and sauce in a separate sauce boat.

In this book, I have tried to stick to the most authentic traditional French cuisine without suggesting too many twists or variations, but this apple sorbet is a slight departure from tradition. I think it works better with the kind of dinners we serve for special occasions these days, which are quite different from how things used to be. Another contemporary addition that works well is the small chunks of strong cheese that we tend to serve as appetizers rather than part of a platter at the end of a meal.

The original trou normand — a shot of Calvados downed in one between the main course and the cheese and/or dessert — was designed to 'burn off' fat and give the sensation of an empty stomach (hence the word 'trou', meaning 'hole' in French) so that people could happily carry on eating copious quantities of food.

Today's version of the trou normand is less brutal on our system and most often consists of an apple sorbet with a splash of Calvados, pear brandy or even cider. Also, as we are more conscious of not over-indulging, even at Christmas, serving a small scoop of tangy sorbet with a splash of top-quality alcohol alongside dessert, or as a digestif with coffee and sweets is much more enjoyable.

Despite the name, the 'hole' doesn't have to be created by something from Normandy. Possible variations include a melon sorbet and a splash of Pineau des Charentes, pineapple with Armagnac, or even blood orange with Cointreau.

Apple sorbet for a 'trou normand'

SERVES 6–8
PREPARATION: 15 MINUTES
CHURNING: 20 MINUTES
FREEZING: 4 HOURS

- 8 Granny Smith apples
- juice of ½ lemon
- 125g (4½oz) apricot jam
- 120g (4¼oz) caster sugar
- 125ml (4fl oz) Calvados

- Peel and core the apples, mixing them with the lemon juice as you go to stop them turning brown. Place with all the other ingredients in a stand mixer bowl and blend to a smooth purée.
- Place the purée in an ice-cream maker and churn for 20 minutes to make a sorbet. Serve immediately or keep in the freezer. You can prepare the purée in advance and make the sorbet at the last minute.
- If you don't have an ice-cream maker, pour the purée into a lidded container and place in the freezer for 2 hours. Remove from the freezer break up the crystals using with an electric whisk. Repeat the freezing and whisking process once more, then freeze until you are ready to serve it.

Yule log

Having clocked up over 30 years' experience making Bûche glacées au chocolat (Yule logs) in France, I have come to the following conclusions:

- If you want a log that is not frozen, you can either order an elaborate one from your trusty local pâtisserie or make a very simple one yourself.
- Opting for a frozen log makes your life easier, especially if you order it in advance from a specialist. However, you can also have fun making one at home. All you need is a few easy-to-find pieces of equipment. This ice cream version is absolute child's play, and children really do love it. I have given you two recipes: one that can be made without an ice-cream maker and a slightly more elaborate sorbet that does require one. You can also follow both recipes to make two separate layers for the same bûche.
- The decorative leaves are very easy to make at home, as long as you can get hold of couverture (coating) chocolate (containing 32–39% cocoa solids and high cocoa butter content for easier handling). You will also need some polycarbonate or plastic chocolate moulds and an angled spatula. No need to temper the chocolate, just keep the leaves in their moulds in the refrigerator until you're ready to serve so that they stay shiny. As for the chocolate mushrooms, I was lucky enough to find them at my local chocolatier. Always make the most of their expertise to decorate your desserts!

Homemade ice cream without an ice-cream maker

MAKES 2 LITRES (3½ PINTS)
PREPARATION: 10 MINUTES
FREEZING: 8 HOURS

- 120g (4¼oz) good-quality cocoa powder
- 200ml (7fl oz) cold water
- 800g (1lb 12oz) sweetened condensed milk
- 1 litre (30fl oz) double cream
- 200g (7oz) good-quality dark chocolate (at least 70% cocoa solids), finely chopped or grated

Admittedly very sweet, but that's what gives this ice cream its silky texture! Buy good-quality dark chocolate and chop it into thin shards so that it melts more easily.

- Put the cocoa powder in a saucepan with the water. Place over a medium heat, stirring with a whisk until the cocoa has dissolved.
- Place the mixture in a large bowl, add the condensed milk and cream and beat until smooth and evenly combined.
- Add the chopped chocolate, stirring to incorporate it into the cream.
- Fill your mould(s), pressing down firmly with the ice cream so it takes the shape of the mould. Leave in the freezer for at least 8 hours.

Chocolate sorbet using an ice-cream maker

MAKES 2 LITRES (3½ PINTS)
PREPARATION: 10 MINUTES
CHURNING: 20 MINUTES
CHILLING: OVERNIGHT
FREEZING: OVERNIGHT

- 900ml (30fl oz) mineral water
- 400g (14oz) caster sugar
- 160g (5¾oz) good-quality cocoa powder
- 500g (1lb 2oz) very good-quaity dark chocolate (at least 70% cocoa solids), broken into chunks

---

- Two days before the sorbet is required, place all the ingredients, except the chocolate, in a saucepan and bring to the boil. Whisk until smooth.
- Remove from the heat and add the chocolate chunks. Allow to melt for a few minutes, then stir again.
- Blend with a stick blender until smooth: chocolate doesn't like water, so you need to blend it to remove any lumps.
- Leave the sorbet to stand overnight in the refrigerator before putting it through the ice-cream maker the following day for 20 minutes.
- Transfer to a silicone mould or lidded container and freeze overnight.

Chocolate mendiants

SERVES 8
PREPARATION: 10 MINUTES
STANDING: 20 MINUTES

- 200g (7oz) couverture (coating) chocolate (see page 130)
- 50g (1¾oz) candied orange peel
- 20g (¾oz) raisins
- 30g (1oz) blanched almonds
- 20g (¾oz) green pistachio nuts

Mendiants, along with truffles, are an essential part of the Christmas chocolate collection in France.

- Place a sheet of baking paper on a cold, smooth surface (marble is perfect for this, but you can also use a metal tray that has been in the refrigerator beforehand).
- Melt the chocolate gently in a bain-marie (a heatproof bowl set over a pan of simmering water) or in a microwave (giving it 20–30 second bursts on medium power) and stirring frequently.
- Place 1 teaspoon of the melted chocolate on your cold surface and spread it out with the back of the spoon to form a small disc. Do this in batches of four or five at a time. Place the dried fruits and nuts on each disc, pressing down gently so they sink into the hot chocolate.
- Repeat this process, reheating the chocolate if necessary.
- Leave the mendiants to cool and harden in a cold place, or even in the refrigerator if you are making them on the morning of your lunch.

Chocolate truffles

SERVES 8–10
PREPARATION: 5 MINUTES
CHILLING: 3–4 HOURS
SHAPING: 10 MINUTES

- 250ml (9fl oz) whipping cream
- 450g (1lb) good-quality dark chocolate (at least 70% cocoa solids)
- 3–4 tablespoons good-quality cocoa powder

- Bring the cream to the boil, then remove from the heat and add the chocolate. Leave it to melt for a few minutes before stirring until smooth. Set this ganache aside in the refrigerator for a few hours to let it cool and harden.
- Spread the cocoa powder on a plate. Using a teaspoon, take a scoop of ganache, place between your palms and roll into a ball. Roll it in the cocoa powder and set aside on a platter. Continue this process until all the ganache has been used.
- Set aside in a cool place before serving. The truffles will keep in the refrigerator for up to 3 days.

Lunch for the little ones

What we think of as a country lunch couldn't be more different from a dinner in town. A country lunch conjures up visions of freedom, relaxation and all the generations together. However, that doesn't mean you should neglect to welcome all your guests properly, and that includes children. My children are grown up now and for the time being I have only one grandchild, Louis, so family lunches with lots of little ones are not yet a thing.

That doesn't stop me from thinking about what would need to be done differently when a lunch involves families with several kids. Are the parents going to turn up with lots of equipment that requires extra space in the kitchen or bedrooms? Perhaps there are food likes, dislikes or allergies to consider? Unless it's a meal with people you know very well, the general rule is that the parents should let the host know in advance of any dietary requirements and if they're bringing any special equipment or food. A quick phone call to ensure everyone's peace of mind would be welcome.

When my French children reached the age where they could feed themselves without needing help, we would simply set a table not too far away from the adults' one, or at least let them leave the table during the meal and come back for dessert. Even if I was a stickler for my children tasting everything, making them sit at a large table when they didn't want to quickly became a nuisance for everyone. It was much better to let them run around and enjoy the countryside – after all, we were not in a restaurant, which was an entirely different scenario!

In case of bad weather, providing a space with toys and games is a nice idea, as is a good film in a room where it can't be heard from the table. The latter might not please all parents, but it does ensure peace and quiet for the grown-ups as the wine flows and they tuck into the cheese and fruit.

Plan the same menu for everyone (except for babies or those with food intolerances, of course), always including simply cooked vegetables and fruit, and perhaps a little extra bread for fussy eaters who won't touch anything!

For very large gatherings, a babysitter for a few hours wouldn't go amiss, and for the very little ones, a room or at least a quiet corner with baby-changing facilities and somewhere they can take a nap would be a very nice touch.

Autumn–winter menu

We have now reached the wintry part of this book, with its rich, warming dishes that fill the house with delicious aromas and make both being in the kitchen and around the table such a pleasurable experience. These recipes are inspired by France's culinary heritage and celebrate its simple, familiar and family-orientated traditions. Rest assured that with a beautifully laid table, a roaring fire in the hearth or even a brazier outside on a sunny autumn day, your guests will enjoy these recipes like a reunion with old friends. Choose the ingredients carefully, especially the meat.

Kirsch
LA DAME BLANCHE RUISSEAU

Rabbit in mustard

SERVES 6
PREPARATION: 3 MINUTES
COOKING: 45–50 MINUTES

- 1 large rabbit, cut into pieces
- 100g (3½oz) Dijon mustard
- 100g (3½oz) butter
- 2 tablespoons olive oil
- 300ml (10fl oz) dry white wine
- 200ml (7fl oz) double cream or 2–3 tablespoons crème fraîche
- salt and pepper

I prefer this version, cooked in a roasting tray rather than a casserole dish, because it makes the mustard flavour intensify before the cream is added to make it milder. It's a tried-and-tested classic.

- Preheat the oven to 200°C (400°F), Gas Mark 6.
- Season the rabbit with salt and pepper, brush with half the mustard, then place in a roasting tray with the butter and oil.
- Roast for 30 minutes, basting from time to time with the cooking juices and melted butter.
- Remove the dish from the oven and pour in the wine, scraping the bottom of the tray to deglaze it.
- Return to the oven for a further 15–20 minutes. Check the rabbit is cooked (it should be milky white, not pink). Transfer it to a plate and keep warm.
- Heat the cooking juices over a low–medium heat, scraping the bottom of the tray again. Add the remaining mustard and the cream, then adjust the seasoning if necessary. Pour the sauce over the rabbit pieces to serve.

TIP
Serve with mashed potatoes (see page 159) or a mixture of mashed carrots and parsnips.

PARIS

Black pudding with apples

SERVES 6
PREPARATION: 10 MINUTES
COOKING: 25 MINUTES

- 8–10 large apples, peeled, cored and quartered
- 50g (1¾oz) butter
- 6 individual black puddings or a 1.2–1.5kg (2lb 10oz–3lb 5oz) large black pudding
- salt and pepper
- mustard, to serve

What could be more comforting and more rooted in the Normandy terroir – which for me is not only home, but also the birthplace of what I consider to be the best French comfort food, with its cream, butter and cheeses – than this very simple dish? Choose your apples well: they should be fairly firm and slightly acidic. Pixie, Elstar, Cox's Orange Pippin, Russet or Galaxy apples would be perfect.

- Place the apples in a saucepan with a small quantity of water. Heat, then, as soon as you see a lot of steam, stir, reduce the heat and cover. Leave the apples to stew for 5 minutes while you cook the black pudding.
- Heat the butter in a non-stick frying pan and brown the black pudding(s) on both sides. Reduce the heat and continue cooking, flipping over from time to time, for around 10 minutes.
- Serve the crisp black pudding(s) with the soft apples and the mustard on the side.

Herb butter
for frogs' legs and snails

SERVES 6
PREPARATION: 5 MINUTES
COOKING: 10–15 MINUTES
CHILLING: 3 HOURS

- 200g (7oz) slightly salted butter, at room temperature
- 3 garlic cloves, peeled
- 2 shallots, peeled and halved
- 1 bunch of flat-leaf parsley
- pepper
- 6 pre-cooked Burgundy snails, in their shells

It's worth having the right equipment to eat the snails: tongs to hold them and small, slender forks to extract the meat. But don't worry, with a healthy appetite you'll manage with a normal fork. For the frogs' legs, just use your fingers.

SNAILS

- Put all the ingredients (except the snails) in a stand mixer and blend together to make a smooth, green butter.
- Place the herb butter on clingfilm and roll it into a log. Seal the ends and set aside in the refrigerator for a few hours.
- Preheat the oven to 200°C (400°F), Gas Mark 6.
- Place the snails in their shells in a suitable dish, add a knob of herb butter to each (and a bit more around the edges for sauce) and bake for 10–15 minutes, until the butter is bubbling and slightly browned around the edges.

TIP

Serve with big chunks of baguette to mop up all the butter.

SERVES 6
COOKING: 10 MINUTES

- 20g (¾oz) butter, for frying
- 24 frogs' legs
- 120g (4¼oz) herb butter (see recipe opposite)
- 1 lemon

FROGS' LEGS

- Heat the butter in a large frying pan and brown the legs. Add the herb butter and allow it to melt around the edges, then stir into the frogs' legs.
- Serve piping hot with a little lemon juice.

Savoyarde fondue for Halloween

SERVES 6
PREPARATION: 25 MINUTES
COOKING: 15–20 MINUTES

- 300g (10½oz) Beaufort cheese
- 300g (10½oz) Comté cheese
- 150g (5½oz) Emmental, Gruyère or Abondance cheese
- 1 garlic clove, peeled
- 200–250ml (7–9fl oz) dry white wine from Savoy (Apremont, Crépy, Chignin...)
- pinch of nutmeg
- pinch of pepper
- 2 tablespoons kirsch
- 1 tablespoon cornflour (optional)
- 1–2 pumpkins, insides hollowed out, to serve

But seriously, folks, what else? I've never understood the appeal of the terrifying boiling oil in a fondue bourguignonne (meat fondue). The cheese version, served in adorable pumpkins at a time of the year when we just want to be indoors, is so wonderful.

- Remove the cheese rinds and grate the remainder.
- Rub the inside of a heavy-based saucepan or fondue pot with the peeled garlic clove. Pour in the white wine, bring to the boil, then reduce the heat to a simmer.
- Add the cheese to the wine a handful at a time, stirring as you do so. Add the nutmeg, pepper and kirsch (also add the garlic clove if you'd like to enhance the flavour). To stabilize the fondue and prevent the cheese mixture from splitting, you can mix the cornflour in a little water and add it at this stage.
- Stir with a wooden spoon, making figure-of-eight shapes until the fondue is smooth and shiny. Transfer to the pumpkins to serve.

TIP

Serve with chunks of slightly stale bread, which provides a crunchy contrast to the cheese and absorbs it better than soft, fresh bread.

Celeriac remoulade with smoked duck breast

SERVES 6
PREPARATION: 20 MINUTES

- 1kg (2lb 4oz) celeriac
- 1 teaspoon lemon juice
- 2 tablespoons Dijon mustard
- 2 egg yolks
- ½ tablespoon neutral oil (grapeseed, rapeseed, etc.)
- 1 teaspoon white wine vinegar or cider
- 2 tablespoons crème fraîche
- salt and pepper

TO SERVE

- 2–3 tablespoons capers
- 2 tablespoons chopped flat-leaf parsley (optional)
- 100–150g (3½–5½oz) smoked duck breast, sliced

This fresh and crunchy dish, which often looks so sad on French supermarket and deli shelves, is much better when homemade. I'm not against using pre-prepared celeriac but a homemade sauce makes all the difference.

- Grate the celeriac into a bowl. Pour in the lemon juice and stir well to stop the celeriac turning brown.
- Using a whisk, mix the mustard and egg yolks together in a separate bowl. Pour in a few drops of oil and whisk to emulsify. Gradually add the rest of the oil, continuing to whisk vigorously to make a mayonnaise.
- Once it is nice and thick, add the vinegar, crème fraîche, salt and pepper.
- Mix the mayonnaise into the grated celeriac and serve topped with the capers, parsley (if you like) and slices of duck breast.

Sausages, mashed potato and onion sauce

SERVES 6
PREPARATION: 15 MINUTES
COOKING: 50 MINUTES

- 6 large Toulouse sausages
- neutral oil (sunflower, grapeseed, etc.), for frying

FOR THE SAUCE

- 3 tablespoons grapeseed oil
- 4 large onions, peeled and finely chopped
- 1 bouquet garni (bay leaf, thyme, rosemary)
- 1 tablespoon red wine
- 300ml (10fl oz) veal or beef stock
- ½ teaspoon cornflour, dissolved in 1 tablespoon water
- salt and pepper

FOR THE MASH

- 1.5kg (3lb 5oz) potatoes (Desiree, King Edward, Maris Piper or similar), peeled and chopped into pieces
- 100g (3½oz) slightly salted butter
- 200ml (7fl oz) whole milk
- salt and pepper

Made well, this basic dish becomes a gourmet delight. Take care with the sauce, making sure to caramelize the onions thoroughly, and pamper your potatoes. Heavenly!

- Start by preparing the sauce: place the oil in a large frying pan over a low heat. When hot, add the onions along with the bouquet garni. Season lightly with salt and pepper. Cook slowly for 40 minutes (yes, really!), stirring to make sure the onions don't stick. Add a splash of water if they start to dry out. Once the onions are browned, deglaze the pan with the red wine and stir again. Pour in the stock and the cornflour liquid and leave to simmer for 5 minutes to thicken the sauce. Set aside.
- For the mash, boil, or preferably steam, the potatoes. Drain them and dry by shaking the saucepan for a few seconds if you have boiled them in water. Mash with a potato masher. Add the knobs of butter and let it melt in. Heat the milk and mix it into the potatoes, adding salt and pepper and stirring gently to obtain a smooth mash. Set aside and keep warm.
- In a cast-iron pan, brown the sausages in a little oil on all sides over a medium heat. You can then continue cooking them either in the oven at 180°C (350°F), Gas Mark 4, or on the hob, regularly turning them, for 10–15 minutes. Once the sausages are nice and crisp on the outside, remove from the pan, then pour in the onion sauce and scrape up the tasty brown bits stuck to the bottom.
- Place a sausage and some mash on each plate, making a small well in the potato to hold the sauce.

Farmhouse pork and cabbage stew

SERVES 6
PREPARATION: 15 MINUTES
SOAKING: 4–5 HOURS
COOKING: 2½ HOURS

- 800g (1lb 12oz) mild cured pork shoulder
- 1 leek, cleaned and chopped
- 3 carrots, peeled and cut into pieces
- 1 onion, peeled
- 2 turnips, peeled and cut into 2 or 3 pieces
- 2 cloves
- 1 bay leaf
- 2 large Morteau sausages
- ½ head of green cabbage, washed and cut into 3 or 4 wedges
- 3 or 4 potatoes, peeled and cut into 3 or 4 pieces

This is simplicity itself: serve on its own with strong mustard or mustard mixed with crème fraîche.

- Soak the pork shoulder in cold water for 4–5 hours, changing the water after about 2 hours.
- Put all the ingredients, except the sausages, cabbage and potatoes, in a large saucepan. Cover with cold water, bring to the boil, then cover and simmer for 1½ hours.
- Add the cabbage and cook for a further 30 minutes.
- Finally, add the sausages and potatoes and cook for 30 minutes. And it's ready!
- Remove the vegetables and the meat, cut up the pork and sausages and arrange everything nicely in a large dish. Serve the broth separately.

Broad bean cassoulet with confit duck

SERVES 6
PREPARATION: 10 MINUTES
COOKING: 40 MINUTES

- 500ml (18fl oz) chicken stock
- 3kg (6lb 8oz) frozen shelled broad beans
- 1 teaspoon fresh thyme
- 200g (7oz) smoked bacon lardons
- 6 large confit duck legs, at room temperature
- salt and pepper

This super-simple but more colourful and spring-like version of cassoulet – the great classic from south-west France – is just crying out to be made at home.

- Bring the chicken stock to the boil, add the broad beans and fresh thyme and cook for 4–6 minutes.
- Meanwhile, brown the bacon lardons in a frying pan.
- Drain the broad beans (making sure to keep half a mugful of the stock), mix with the lardons and place in a large ovenproof earthenware dish or roasting tin. Pour in the stock.
- Preheat the oven to 180°C (350°F), Gas Mark 4.
- Remove the duck legs from their packaging and place them on top of the beans, with the equivalent of 2 tablespoons of the fat that surrounds them.
- Heat and brown in the oven for 10–15 minutes. The duck skin and edges of the dish should be crisp and the beans tasty and tender. Season if needed. Serve piping hot.

Neck of lamb with carrots and red wine

SERVES 6
PREPARATION: 20–25 MINUTES
COOKING: 1¼ HOURS

- 2 tablespoons olive oil
- 12–15 pieces of lamb neck
- 30g (1oz) smoked pork belly, cut into lardons
- 2 onions, peeled and sliced
- 2 garlic cloves, peeled and finely chopped
- 4 carrots, peeled and chopped into pieces
- 1 heaped tablespoon plain flour
- 1 bottle of full-bodied red wine
- 1 bouquet garni (bay leaf, thyme, rosemary)
- salt and pepper

Use shoulder of lamb if you prefer, but I like the really rustic side to cuts of lamb neck on the bone. This dish tastes even better reheated.

- Preheat the oven to 150°C (300°F), Gas Mark 2.
- Heat the oil in a cast-iron saucepan or sauté pan, then brown the pieces of meat on all sides. Remove them and set aside.
- Fry the lardons until crisp and brown, then add the onions and sweat for a few minutes before adding the garlic. Cook for a minute, then add the carrots and mix.
- Return the meat to the pan, add the flour and cook for 1–2 minutes over a medium heat, stirring constantly.
- Pour in the red wine, scraping up the bits in the bottom of the pan, then add the bouquet garni, season lightly and bring to the boil.
- Cover and braise for about 1¼ hours. Check the cooking after 1 hour.

TIP
Serve piping hot with some delicious mashed potatoes (see page 159).

Mussels
with saffron and cumin

SERVES 6
PREPARATION: 15 MINUTES
COOKING: 20 MINUTES

- 30g (1oz) butter
- 2 shallots, peeled and finely chopped
- 200ml (7fl oz) dry white wine
- 2kg (4lb 8oz) mussels, thoroughly scrubbed and rinsed
- 200ml (7fl oz) double cream or crème fraîche
- generous pinch of saffron threads
- ½–1 teaspoon ground cumin, according to taste
- pepper

A slightly decadent and exotic way to serve our otherwise traditional mussels.

- Heat the butter in a large saucepan. Add the shallots and let them sweat for a few minutes. Pour in the wine and bring to the boil over a medium heat. Throw the mussels in, give the pan a good shake and turn up the heat. Cover with a lid so that the mussels steam.
- Meanwhile, heat the cream, add the saffron and cumin and leave to infuse.
- Once the mussels have all opened (discard any that haven't), add the cream and stir well to coat the mussels. Season with pepper.
- Serve straight away, piping hot.

TIP
Garnish with a little flat-leaf parsley and/or fresh coriander and serve with fresh bread.

Floating islands with pink praline

SERVES 6
PREPARATION: 25 MINUTES
COOKING: 15 MINUTES
CHILLING: 2 HOURS

FOR THE CUSTARD

- 500ml (18fl oz) whole milk
- seeds from 1 vanilla pod
- 5 egg yolks
- 70g (2½oz) caster sugar

FOR THE FLOATING ISLANDS

- 3 egg whites
- 30g (1oz) icing sugar
- 100g (3½oz) crushed pink pralines

Ever so pretty, slightly crunchy, the perfect dessert for a Sunday lunch.

- Start with the custard: pour the milk into a saucepan, add the vanilla seeds and bring to boiling point (without letting it boil!). Beat the egg yolks in a bowl with the sugar until they double in volume and turn pale.
- Pour the milk over the yolk mixture, stir gently, then return to the saucepan over a medium heat. Stir constantly with a wooden spoon. When the cream thickens and your finger leaves a track on the back of the spoon, remove from the heat and pour immediately into a mixing bowl to halt the cooking process.
- Leave to cool for 2 hours in the refrigerator before pouring it into your serving dish(es).
- To make the islands, whisk the egg whites into stiff peaks, then fold in the icing sugar in 2–3 batches. Once the mixture is shiny and firm, gently fold in 1–2 tablespoons of praline.
- Spoon small mounds of the meringue onto a plate. Microwave for just under 1 minute at 800W: you'll see the islands rise. Remove from the microwave, then leave to cool.
- Arrange the islands on top of the custard. Sprinkle over the remaining praline and serve immediately.

Crêpes Suzette

SERVES 6
PREPARATION: 25 MINUTES
COOKING: 20 MINUTES

FOR THE CRÊPES

- 120g (4¼oz) plain flour
- 1 tablespoon caster sugar
- 2 eggs, lightly beaten
- 200ml (7fl oz) whole milk
- grated zest of 1 orange
- 50g (1¾oz) unsalted butter, melted, plus extra for frying

FOR THE SAUCE

- 50g (1¾oz) slightly salted butter
- juice of 3–4 oranges (about 150ml/5fl oz)
- grated zest of 1 orange
- grated zest and juice of 1 lemon
- 1 tablespoon caster sugar
- 3 tablespoons orange liqueur, such as Grand Marnier or Cointreau (optional)

A great classic that requires a little work and lots of care and attention. Most steps can be done well before your guests arrive.

- To make the crêpe batter, sift the flour into a mixing bowl. Add the sugar, make a well in the centre and pour in the lightly beaten eggs. Beat with an electric whisk, then gradually pour in the milk, continuing to beat until the batter is completely smooth. Finally, add the orange zest and measured butter.
- Heat a crêpe pan and use kitchen paper to grease it with a little butter. Pour in a ladleful of batter, tilting the pan so that it covers the entire bottom. Cook the crêpe until the edges start to brown, then slide a spatula underneath and flip it over. Once it is equally browned on the other side, slide it onto a plate and keep warm. Repeat this step, adding a little butter to the pan ech time until you have used all the batter (it should make around 12 crêpes).
- To make the sauce, gently heat the butter in a frying pan, then add all the other ingredients (including the liqueur, if using), stirring with a wooden spoon. Allow the mixture to heat through and simmer gently before placing the first crêpe in the sauce to reheat it.
- Fold the crêpe in half, then again to make a fan shape. Move it to the side of the frying pan and continue with the other crêpes. Carry on until all the crêpes are coated with sauce and folded. Serve them in the pan.

TIP
If you like, you can splash on a little liqueur to flambé the crêpes just before serving.

Fig tiramisu with biscuits roses de Reims

SERVES 6–8
PREPARATION: 15 MINUTES
CHILLING: 3–4 HOURS, IDEALLY OVERNIGHT

- 3 egg yolks
- 4 tablespoons caster sugar
- 400g (14oz) mascarpone cheese
- 1 glass of Marsala or Lillet Rosé
- 1½–2 packets of biscuits rose de Reims, according to the size of your dish
- 8 fresh figs, cut into slices about 1.5cm (⅝in) thick

A slight departure from my almost 100% French repertoire, but tiramisu crossed the border from Italy such a long time ago and, to be fair, this version is made using pretty French pink biscuits from Reims.

- Whisk the egg yolks with the sugar until they turn pale and double in volume. Now add the mascarpone in 2 batches and beat until you have a smooth, sweet cream.
- Pour your chosen alcohol into a bowl. Dip one side of the whole biscuits very quickly (2 seconds!) in it and arrange them in the bottom of a high-sided dish about 3–4cm (1¼–1½in) deep.
- Spread over a third of the cream and top with half the figs. Repeat the process, finishing with the final third of the cream. Cover in clingfilm and set aside in the refrigerator for at least 3–4 hours.
- To serve, crumble 2–3 of the remaining rose de Reims biscuits over the dish.

Rice pudding

SERVES 6
PREPARATION: 10 MINUTES
COOKING: 2 HOURS
CHILLING: 30 MINUTES

Loosely inspired by the traditional rice pudding made at the gourmet bistro L'Ami Jean in Paris. Add flaked almonds and caramelized pecan nuts for some welcome crunch.

- 200g (7oz) Arborio rice
- 1 litre (1¾ pints) whole milk
- 1 vanilla pod, split in half
- 150g (5½oz) caster sugar
- 200ml (7fl oz) custard (see page 172)
- 300ml (10fl oz) chilled whipped cream
- 6 tablespoons salted butter caramel sauce

- Put the rice in a large saucepan with the milk, scrape in the vanilla seeds, then add the pod. Bring to the boil and simmer over a very low heat for about 2 hours (yes, you read it right!), stirring regularly. Add more milk if the rice starts to dry out, because it needs to be creamy.
- Turn off the heat and add the sugar, stirring until completely dissolved. Leave the rice to cool, then mix it into the custard.
- Place the mixture in the refrigerator until it is completely cold.
- Serve with the whipped cream and caramel sauce.

Chocolate mousse with mascarpone

SERVES 6
PREPARATION: 15 MINUTES
COOKING: 2–5 MINUTES
CHILLING: 1 HOUR MINIMUM

- 300g (10½oz) good-quality dark chocolate (at least 70% cocoa solids)
- 150g (5½oz) mascarpone cheese
- 150ml (5fl oz) whipping cream
- 4 egg yolks

- Break the chocolate into pieces and melt very gently in a bain-marie (a heatproof bowl set over a pan of simmering water) or in a microwave (giving it 20–30 second bursts on medium power) and stirring often.
- Whisk the mascarpone with the cream until thick, then add the egg yolks and stir until you obtain a smooth, light mixture. Add the chocolate (keeping 2 tablespoons aside for decoration) and mix until smooth.
- Pour the mousse into a large serving bowl or 4 small bowls. Leave the mousse in the refrigerator for about 1 hour before serving.

Foraging

My friends, when you are foraging, especially for wild mushrooms, make sure you have experts with you. Having been extremely ill after eating some pan-fried 'ceps' which at the time tasted delicious and were served by a well-meaning friend, I now require Sébastian Bras-level expertise before I would eat them again. Trust Only Those Who Know, especially when at 8am on a Sunday morning, for that day's lunch, you can't pop into the pharmacy to get some seemingly innocent-looking chanterelles checked, as you usually would any other day in France.

It requires a fair amount of research, as well as the intelligence to know what you don't know. That said, foraging is a wonderful occupation, and, with a little luck, you'll get to meet some real countryside lovers. And if you're fortunate enough to know people who are passionate about edible and/or medicinal flowers, the world's your oyster (or at least your oyster-flavoured borage plant). That's not to say that even the kindest of people will divulge where their secret foraging spots are, and that's as it should be. Such knowledge has to be earned.

So here is a short basic glossary, a gateway guide to foraging for those who only sporadically experience the joys of the countryside. Although my little glossary isn't extensive and is naturally Franco-centric, it does include lots you can easily pick by the sides of fields and along footpaths and country roads in Europe, all of which will add flavour to your dishes and, most importantly, cannot be confused with a similar plant that would land you in hospital.

Nettle: using gloves, and well away from the road, animals and pesticides, pick the young shoots in spring and use them as you would blanched spinach shoots. Delicious in soups, quiches, pestos and gratins.

Dandelion: same procedure as for nettles, find plants that are well away from the road. The young leaves, picked before the flowers blossom, can be eaten in salads.

Wild garlic: heralds the start of the summer lunch season and it's hard to avoid the excitement in the countryside when this pretty and delicious plant first appears. Everything is edible, the young leaves – much more delicate before the flowers appear – can be used in soups, pestos or simply as a herb, while the flowers themselves can be used for decoration and in condiments, while its buds can be turned into capers. Wild garlic is easy to propagate from a few plants in a shady, damp spot in the garden.

Sweet violet: easy to spot, its scented flowers, with a slightly sweet flavour, are perfect in fruit salads, infused to make cordials or as decoration for cakes and desserts.

Daisy: one of the first spring arivals, its slightly spicy flowers will look perfectly pretty in salads.

Elderflower: pure joy! The beautiful and fleetingly fresh flowers can be eaten whole, in fritters, or infused to make wonderfully fragrant cordials. Later, the purple-black berries can be picked to make juices, cordials and jellies.

Meadowsweet: a little later in the summer, and until early autumn, you can find these large creamy flowers with their downy stems near hedgerows. Infuse them in cream to make delicately perfumed custards or ice creams.

Wild or dog rose: its beautiful, slightly fragrant petals can be used in your early summer salads and cakes.

Easter menu

Easter lunch marks the end of winter, the reawakening of nature and whispers in our ear the promise of delicious meals in the garden. Depending on when Easter falls, sometimes it is possible to set the table outside, even if it means bringing out jumpers and blankets, but most years, we are still indoors. I like to give my table a calm, slightly monastic feel, while my menu, like the rest of this book, is ultra-traditional and features all the usual French suspects – broad beans, asparagus, lamb, chocolate – that we are so happy to discover again at the start of spring. The cooking times are long, as is the preparation, standing and cooling, so you'll need to get started the day before or even earlier. However, this menu will give you plenty of time to set a beautiful table and enjoy the celebration with your family and guests.

Confit shoulder of lamb

SERVES 6–8
PREPARATION: 25 MINUTES
COOKING: 6–7 HOURS
STANDING: 20 MINUTES

- 1 shoulder of lamb, 1.5–2kg (3lb 5oz–4lb 8oz)
- 4–5 garlic cloves, peeled and crushed
- olive oil
- 3 onions, peeled
- 1 bouquet garni (bay leaf, thyme, rosemary)
- 500ml (18fl oz) chicken stock
- salt and pepper

TO SERVE

- Herby broad beans (see page 191)
- Mogette beans with smoked ham (see page 192)

This method of cooking the shoulder, which already has a high collagen content, makes it absolutely melt in the mouth. For more than six guests, it is best to buy two shoulders weighing under 1.5kg (3lb 5oz) each and enjoy the leftovers!

- Preheat the oven to 220°C (425°F), Gas Mark 7.
- Rub the lamb shoulder with 1 garlic clove and a little olive oil and place it on a bed of the onions, garlic and herbs in a high-sided roasting tin. Bake for 30 minutes.
- Remove the tin from the oven, pour on the chicken stock and wrap the dish in kitchen foil to create a kind of steam oven. Reduce the oven temperature to 140 or 150°C (275 or 300°F), Gas Mark 1 or 2 and cook for 5–6 hours. The meat should come away with a spoon.
- Remove the foil, return to the oven and increase the temperature to 180°C (350°F), Gas Mark 4, leaving it to cook for 30 minutes or long enough so the surface of the shoulder is caramelized or crisp.
- Remove from the oven, cover loosely with the foil so the meat does not cool down too much, then leave it to rest for 20 minutes before serving with Herby broad beans and Mogette beans.

Herby broad beans

SERVES 6–8
PREPARATION: 20 MINUTES
COOKING: 10 MINUTES

- 500ml (18fl oz) good-quality vegetable stock
- 2 spring onions, finely chopped
- 1 large handful of fresh herbs (curly parsley, chives, chervil, tarragon)
- 750g (1lb 10oz) frozen shelled broad beans

If you find fresh broad beans and you have time to spare, and perhaps some assistants to help you, that's wonderful. But just like peas, if you have a lot of guests and time is not on your side, there's no shame in buying frozen, ready-shelled broad beans. All you need is a good vegetable stock, fresh herbs and spring onions to turn it into an amazingly tasty dish.

- Bring the stock to the boil and add the broad beans, spring onions and half of the herbs tied together in a bouquet. Cook for 10 minutes until the beans are tender, then drain.
- Discard the cooked herbs but set the spring onions aside. Reduce the stock until you obtain a fairly thick liquid. Mix with the beans and the rest of the freshly chopped spring onions.

Mogette beans with smoked ham

SERVES 6
PREPARATION: 15 MINUTES
SOAKING: OVERNIGHT
COOKING: 1¾ HOURS

- 500g (1lb 2oz) dried mogette beans from the Vendée (white beans or cannellini beans will also work here)
- 1 tablespoon olive oil
- 1 onion, peeled and finely chopped
- 2 garlic cloves, peeled and finely chopped
- 3 carrots, peeled and sliced into rounds
- 100ml (3½fl oz) dry white wine
- 1 bouquet garni (bay leaf, thyme, rosemary)
- 3–4 very thin slices of smoked ham, torn into large pieces
- salt and pepper

This classic dish is usually served with a good thick slice of smoked ham. When I'm making it as a side dish – to accompany lamb, for example – I like to add thin slices of smoked ham at the end of the cooking process to enhance the flavour. Ready-prepared mogette beans are practical and delicious, but dried ones, soaked overnight and cooked slowly over a low heat, give even better results. Remember, do not add salt to the beans at the start of cooking as this can make them tough.

- Soak the beans in cold water overnight.
- In a saucepan, heat the olive oil and fry the onion and garlic, making sure they do not brown. Add the carrots and cook for 3–4 minutes over a medium heat, stirring without caramelizing.
- Add the drained beans, white wine, bouquet garni and pepper.
- Cover with water, then bring to the boil and leave to simmer over a low heat for 1¼ hours, stirring from time to time and adding extra water if necessary.
- At the end of the cooking time, add the slices of ham, then simmer for another 10 minutes. Adjust the seasoning (be careful, the ham is already salty) and serve immediately.

Rabbit in jelly

SERVES 6
PREPARATION: 20 MINUTES
COOKING: 1 HOUR
CHILLING: 4 HOURS, OR OVERNIGHT

- 1 rabbit, cut into 6 or 8 pieces
- 1 bottle dry white wine
- 1 large bouquet garni (tarragon, chervil, thyme, chives)
- 2 carrots, peeled and sliced into rounds
- 2 onions, peeled and finely chopped
- 1 garlic clove, peeled and crushed
- 3 gelatine leaves
- salt and pepper

It seems a bit harsh perhaps, even for those of us who are not vegetarians, to celebrate the birth of spring bunnies and at the same time put them in the cooking pot. This retro Easter dish also works well with chicken, so you have a choice. I love this recipe because I can serve it in my beautiful vintage terrine, and it also keeps well in a cool place, leaving me plenty of free time to spend with my friends.

- Preheat the oven to 150°C (300°F), Gas Mark 2.
- Place all the ingredients, except the gelatine, in a large ovenproof casserole dish, then season lightly with salt and pepper. Bring to the boil on the hob, then cover, and braise in the oven for 1 hour.
- When ready, the rabbit should be tender but still firm. Remove the casserole dish from the oven and take out the rabbit pieces.
- Strain the broth through a sieve, setting the carrots and onions aside.
- Reduce the broth on the hob until you are left with 500ml (18fl oz) of liquid.
- Meanwhile, debone the rabbit, taking care to remove all the tiny pieces of meat. Set aside.
- Leave the reduced stock to cool slightly. Check the seasoning.
- Soak the gelatine leaves in cold water for 5–10 minutes to soften them. Squeeze them dry, then dissolve in a small quantity of stock. Pour this into the remaining stock.
- Arrange the rabbit pieces, carrots and onions in a terrine dish and pour the stock over them.
- Cover with a lid or clingfilm and place in the refrigerator for a minimum of 4 hours, but ideally overnight.

Easter pâté

SERVES 8
PREPARATION: 40 MINUTES
COOKING: 40 MINUTES

- 6 eggs
- 400g (14oz) minced veal (shoulder)
- 400g (14oz) minced pork (shoulder, belly)
- 1 small garlic clove, peeled and finely chopped (optional)
- 2 or 3 shallots, peeled and finely chopped
- 2 tablespoons crème fraîche
- 1 tablespoon olive oil
- 1 large handful of flat-leaf parsley and 1 large handful of chives, finely chopped
- generous pinch of grated nutmeg
- 2 discs or rectangles of puff pastry, depending on the shape of your dish
- salt and pepper

Also known as pâté berrichon, this meaty Easter dish, with hard-boiled eggs symbolizing fertility, marked the end of Lent. Traditionally, this mixture of minced pork and veal was flavoured with port, garlic and shallots, but there are many variations. One friend of mine uses minced beef and sausage meat, for example, while another adds a teaspoon of allspice. Personally, I avoid adding too much garlic because it tends to dominate the flavours when cooked. I prefer fresh herbs with a pinch of nutmeg. Often seen in the form of a large flattened sausage, the pâté can also be put in a pie dish, providing a larger surface area for pretty pastry decorations.

- Place 4 of the eggs in a saucepan of cold water and cook for 10 minutes from the moment you turn on the heat.
- Preheat the oven to 200°C (400°F), Gas Mark 6. Line your pie dish with baking paper if you want to remove the pie later for serving.
- Mix all the other ingredients together, apart from the puff pastry and 1 egg. Knead well until you have a smooth filling.
- Line your dish with 1 piece of pastry, letting it overhang the edge. Spoon in the filling and spread smoothly.
- Peel the eggs and cut them in half lengthways. Press them, cut-side down, into the filling in a circle.
- Brush water around the edge of the pastry, then trim off the excess, saving the offcuts for decoration. Cover the filling with the second piece of pastry, trim neatly, then press around the edge with a fork.
- Reroll the offcuts, then cut decorative shapes from them. Beat the remaining egg with a little water and use some to stick the decorations to the top of the pie. Brush the rest of the beaten egg all over the surface so it will develop a nice glaze.
- Bake for 40 minutes on the middle shelf of the oven. If the top begins to brown too much, reduce the temperature slightly and cover the pie with foil. When ready, serve hot or warm.

TIP
Accompany with a green salad and fresh herbs.

Asparagus tart

SERVES 6
PREPARATION: 15 MINUTES
COOKING: 30–35 MINUTES

- 1 sheet of ready-rolled puff pastry
- 1 egg, beaten
- 7 or 8 green asparagus spears
- 300g (10½oz) soft goats' cheese
- olive oil
- 50g (1¾oz) raw ham slices (preferably prosciutto), torn
- 3 spring onions, trimmed and chopped
- fresh thyme

A pretty tart that looks good as a starter and is light enough to serve before your guests tuck into the lamb, especially if you're not keen on serving the hearty Easter pâté (see page 199).

Tha tart would also be nice as an appetizer with pre-dinner drinks were it not for the fact that the asparagus makes it somewhat impractical as finger food. It is best served in the traditional manner, at table with plates and cutlery.

- Preheat the oven to 180°C (350°F), Gas Mark 4.
- Score around the pastry with a knife 2cm (¾in) from the edge, as if drawing a frame. Be careful not to cut through the pastry.
- Brush the beaten egg all over the pastry, then prick the frame with a fork to prevent it from rising. Bake for 15 minutes to brown it. Set aside.
- Steam the asparagus for about 8 minutes, until tender but still firm. Cut them in half lengthways.
- Mix the goats' cheese with a little olive oil to make a soft paste, then spread over the centre of the cooled pastry. Place the asparagus halves on top, alternating the inner and outer sides.
- Sprinkle pieces of ham, chopped spring onions and thyme over the tart.
- Bake for 10 minutes until everything is lightly browned and crisp.
- Serve hot, warm or cold.

Easter lamala

MAKES 1 CAKE
PREPARATION: 25 MINUTES
COOKING: 35 MINUTES

- 20g (¾oz) butter
- 100g (3½oz) sifted plain flour, plus 1 tablespoon for dusting
- 3 eggs, separated
- 150g (5½oz) caster sugar
- 1 sachet (7–8g) vanilla sugar (or ½ teaspoon vanilla paste or seeds from ½ vanilla pod)
- icing sugar, to serve

Traditionally in Alsace, the Easter lamb is represented as a light brioche or sponge cake cooked in a lamb-shaped clay or earthenware mould called a lamala in the Upper Rhine region, or a lammele in the Lower Rhine. I found my more basic non-stick metal mould very easily online, but if you can get your hands on an old earthenware one, go ahead and use it. You'll need to grease and flour it thoroughly to ensure the features, nose and ears of the lamb are visible. For a large number of guests, make a small flock and serve with the first strawberries of the season, which are always welcome even though they are not yet at their peak.

- Preheat the oven to 180°C (350°F), Gas Mark 4. Melt the butter and carefully brush it inside your mould (see above). Sprinkle with a dusting of flour and set aside.
- Beat the egg whites into soft peaks, using a whisk or an electric mixer. Add half the caster sugar and beat again until the whites are shiny and firm.
- In another bowl, beat the yolks with the rest of the caster sugar and the vanilla sugar until they turn white and double in volume. Gently fold the mixtures together, using a spatula to lift up the mixture and keep it as light as possible.
- Gently fold in the flour with the spatula. When it is well incorporated, pour the mixture into the two halves of mould, close with the clips and bake for 35 minutes. The sponge mixture will seep out a bit but don't worry!
- Leave to cool completely before turning out.
- Dust with icing sugar and serve.

Rich chocolate cake

SERVES 6–8
PREPARATION: 30 MINUTES
COOKING: 30 MINUTES
STANDING: OVERNIGHT

- 225g (8oz) plain flour
- 2 heaped teaspoons baking powder
- 225g (8oz) slightly salted butter, at room temperature, plus extra for greasing
- 200g (7oz) light brown muscovado sugar
- 1 teaspoon vanilla extract
- 4 large eggs

FOR THE ICING

- 200g (7oz) good-quality dark chocolate (at least 70% cocoa solids)
- 250g (9oz) unsalted butter, at room temperature
- 250g (9oz) icing sugar, sifted
- 1 teaspoon vanilla extract

TIP
Decorate with chocolate sprinkles or other Easter chocolates just before serving.

I love the flavour and texture of muscovado sugar in cakes and pastries, and when paired with chocolate, it's divine. Use the best chocolate you can find and leave the cake to stand overnight before icing and serving. It will taste even better.

- The day before, preheat the oven to 180°C (350°F), Gas Mark 4. Grease 2 round, shallow cake tins, 22cm (8½in), and line with baking paper.
- Sift and mix the flour and baking powder. Beat the softened butter with the sugar for 4–5 minutes, until the mixture is pale and fluffy. Add the vanilla, then stir in the eggs one by one, scraping the sides of the bowl as you go. Once all the eggs have been added, gradually add the flour mixture and beat together quickly.
- Pour the mixture into the cake tins, then bake for 35 minutes, checking after 25 minutes. When a skewer or the blade of a knife inserted in the centre of the cakes comes out clean, set aside to cool for a few minutes, before turning onto a wire rack and leaving them to cool completely.
- Leave to rest overnight in a cool place, not the refrigerator.
- On the day you want to ice the cake, gently melt the chocolate in a bain-marie (a heatproof bowl set over a pan of simmering water) or in a microwave (giving it 20–30 second bursts on medium power) and stirring frequently. Set aside to cool. Beat the butter with the icing sugar and vanilla until you obtain a smooth and fluffy consistency. Fold in the chocolate with a spatula until everything is well combined and shiny.
- Spread a quarter to one-third of the icing between the cakes to sandwich them together, then cover the top and sides with the rest of the mixture. Smooth over the surface and decorate as you wish (see Tip).

Chocolate pots

SERVES 6–8
PREPARATION: 10 MINUTES
CHILLING: 2–3 HOURS

- 150g (5½oz) very good-quality dark chocolate (at least 70% cocoa solids)
- 250ml (9fl oz) double cream
- 2 egg yolks beaten with 2 tablespoons water (or cognac, Cointreau, etc.)
- 20g (¾oz) slightly salted butter, softened

It's hard to give exact quantities here because it depends largely on the size of dishes you use for serving. Personally, I love tiny porcelain pots and tiny spoons. This means you can savour the rich chocolate ganache more slowly, leaving room for the chocolate eggs you've pilfered from the kids.

- Break the chocolate into small pieces and place in a heatproof bowl.
- Bring the cream just to the boil, then quickly pour it over the chocolate and leave it for 2–3 minutes.
- Stir gently until you obtain a smooth, shiny ganache. Leave to cool a little more so that the ganache is still warm, but not hot enough to cook the eggs. Stir them in, then immediately add the softened butter in small pieces.
- Stir until the butter is mixed in and your ganache is smooth.
- Pour into small pots or glasses and cover in clingfilm before placing in the refrigerator to rest for 2–3 hours.

TIP
Serve cold with langues-de-chat biscuits.

Shopping at the market

No my friends, your most important piece of equipment when you go to the market isn't your chic designer basket, it's your shopping list! If you are having guests to lunch, you need to plan ahead. And for me – as someone who already lives in a kind of parallel universe of moments shared with others – imagining new dishes, table decoration and seating plans are probably the things I enjoy the most about entertaining.

Very few of us have the talent and devil-may-care attitude (seemingly baked into so many French cooks' DNA) that are needed to devise a lunch menu on the spot while shopping at the market in the morning, 2–3 hours before the guests arrive. Although this might occasionally prove necessary for last-minute lunches, these often end up being the most joyful and creative kind because they give us an excuse to experiment, take shortcuts and even make mistakes. That's why I believe it is so important and valuable to master a few French basics that will please everyone. Throughout this book, I share recipes and tips on chicken, cheese, eggs and tarts, organized by theme. These are the recipes that ensure you'll always be prepared when time and inspiration are lacking. After all, you'll always be able to find a good-quality chicken, seasonal fruits for a tart, eggs for a chocolate mousse or oeufs à la neige, vegetables to roast or cook as a gratin, and, of course, everything you need to put together a good cheese course. Decorate your table nicely and, unless your guests happen to be the kind of people who think that the dining table is a MasterChef performance and feel it's okay to judge everything, they will thank you for the simple and delicious dishes you have made them.

(Continued on page 219)

ordre, beauté, Luxe calme et volupté

NIKE

Generally speaking, however, if you want a pretty and well laid-out table and/or garden, with a delicious menu that leaves you time to spend with your guests, you need to plan ahead and prepare. Ideally, this means shopping the day before, at the Saturday morning market for Sunday lunch, for example. In Le Perche (where I live), we are lucky enough to have the wonderful Mortagne market. It's the perfect size and the market stalls are set out right next to craft boutiques or inside the covered market halls.

Take the time to think about your menu (which should of course be as seasonal as possible) but also about the presentation. The crockery you use can be the starting point – the beautiful soup tureen bought in the second-hand shop is crying out for a seasonal soup, those pale green vintage plates would be perfect for serving oysters, the blue and white floral fruit bowl is just waiting to be filled with strawberries and raspberries. Setting the table is my usual starting point before I have even begun cooking.

Bar à Chocolat
Salon de thé
Biscuiterie
Produits chocolatés
Boissons fraîches
RUE
du CHÂTEAU

Summer menus

The first of my two summer menus is for a lunch for six people, with dishes served at the table rather than buffet style. In other words, it's a little more formal. The table setting is almost as important as what I am cooking, so I've matched the table and food harmoniously in a red, white and blue colour scheme. Everything is warm, cold or chilled, light but full of flavour, and can all be prepared in advance so that the person doing the cooking stays cool when the daytime temperature rises. It's such a pleasure to be in the kitchen early in the morning at the height of summer, preparing and planning for the time I'll spend with my family and friends. In this section, you'll notice even more recipes in the 'let's rehabilitate frozen food' series because, frankly, why cook a dish and then freeze it when good minimally processed frozen ingredients already exist?

Piquillo pepper brandade

SERVES 6
PREPARATION: 10 MINUTES

- 750g (1lb 10oz) good-quality cod brandade
- 1 tablespoon crème fraîche
- 1–2 tablespoons chopped chives or flat-leaf parsley
- 12–18 piquillo peppers from a jar, drained
- olive oil, for drizzling

- Put the cod brandade in a mixing bowl with the crème fraîche and chopped herbs and mix together to soften.
- Fill the piquillos with the brandade mixture, taking care not to overfill them, then wipe the surface of the peppers clean.
- Pack them tightly in a large dish and leave to rest in a cool place.
- Just before serving, drizzle with a few drops of olive oil.

Very lazy cold tomato soup

SERVES 6–8
PREPARATION: 25 MINUTES
CHILLING: 1–2 HOURS

FOR THE CROUTONS

- 6 slices of rustic bread
- 2 garlic cloves, peeled and halved
- olive oil
- sea salt flakes

FOR THE SOUP

- 1 litre (1¾ pints) shop-bought gazpacho soup, fresh or frozen
- 500g (1lb 2oz) good-quality ready-made tomato sauce with olive oil, fresh or frozen
- olive oil
- juice of 1 lemon
- salt and pepper

TO SERVE

- ice cubes
- fresh basil

- Start by making the croutons: preheat the oven to 180°C (350°F), Gas Mark 4. Rub the slices of bread with the halved garlic cloves. Cut or tear the bread into pieces and place them in an ovenproof baking tray. Drizzle with olive oil and sprinkle on a few sea salt flakes. Using your hands, mix the croutons so they are well seasoned.
- Transfer to the oven for a few minutes to brown, keeping a close eye on them. Set aside.
- To prepare the soup: combine the gazpacho and tomato sauce in a large bowl and place in the refrigerator to chill thoroughly, for 1–2 hours. (If using frozen, defrost to a liquid but still cold.) Before serving, check the seasoning and, if necessary, add olive oil, lemon juice, salt and pepper.
- Serve in a pretty soup tureen with a few ice cubes and basil leaves, and serve the croutons in a separate dish.

Tomato and anchovy tart

SERVES 6
PREPARATION: 10 MINUTES
COOKING: 20–25 MINUTES

- 5 or 6 salted anchovies
- 3–4 tablespoons sun-dried tomatoes
- 400g (14oz) ready-made pizza dough or 1 pack puff pastry
- plain flour, for dusting
- 2 or 3 firm fresh tomatoes
- olive oil, for drizzling
- handful of black olives
- fresh basil leaves, to garnish

- Preheat the oven to 200°C (400°F), Gas Mark 6.
- Mix half the anchovies into the sun-dried tomatoes, crushing them well.
- Roll out the dough or pastry on a floured work surface and use to line a 22–24cm (8½–9½ inch) tart dish.
- Slice the fresh tomatoes very thinly and arrange them in a single layer on the dough. Drizzle with olive oil, add the remaining anchovy pieces and the olives, then bake for 20–25 minutes, until the edge of the tart is well-browned and the tomatoes are slightly crisp around their edges.
- Remove from the oven, sprinkle over some basil leaves, then serve the tart hot, warm or cold.

Go-to tartines

Once again, what we are making here is not haute cuisine, but it is eminently practical. Here are two recipes that I have always found useful. To add extra crunch, you can also add nuts such as almonds, hazelnuts and peanuts. Or even sesame paste to make it more like a traditional hummus.

PEA TARTINES

SERVES 6–8
COOKING: 5 MINUTES
CHILLING: 10 MINUTES
PREPARATION: 2 MINUTES

- 300g (10½oz) frozen peas
- 1 small garlic clove, peeled
- grated zest of 1 lemon
- 1 tablespoon lemon juice
- 1 tablespoon fresh herbs (chives, basil, chervil, tarragon or a mixture)
- olive oil, for drizzling
- 300g (10½oz) cream cheese
- slices of toast
- salt and pepper

Despite their annoying tendency to escape from the bag and spend years in the bottom of the freezers frozen peas are our faithful friends in the kitchen. I could write a whole book of life-saving pea recipes, but for our country lunches in the sun, here's one that can be used as a delicious alternative to a starter and is easy to serve to guests.

- Cook the peas in boiling water for 2 minutes. Drain and set aside 1–2 tablespoons. Put the rest of the peas, together with the garlic, lemon zest and juice, herbs and olive oil in your stand mixer and blend to a fairly firm paste. Adjust the texture with olive oil. Season, spread the cream cheese on the toast and top with the pea mixture. Garnish with the reserved whole peas.

CHICKPEA TARTINES WITH FRESH PEPPERS AND ESPELETTE CHILLI PEPPER

SERVES 6–8

- 400g (14oz) canned chickpeas, drained
- 1 small garlic clove, peeled
- 1 teaspoon lemon juice
- 1 or 2 roasted red peppers from a jar (depending on size, you don't want the paste to be too runny), plus ½ roasted red pepper to garnish
- 1 teaspoon Espelette chilli pepper
- olive oil and/or lemon juice
- 300g (10½oz) cream cheese
- slices of toast
- salt and pepper

Just like frozen peas, certain canned or preserved foods can come to your rescue. Admittedly a lot less refined (and tasty) than their dried and soaked equivalents, canned chickpeas are a great base for hummus-adjacent recipes that everyone loves.

- Place all the ingredients (except the cream cheese and bread) in your stand mixer and blend to a coarse paste. Adjust the texture with olive oil and/or lemon juice. Season.
- Spread the cream cheese on the toasts and top with the chickpea mixture. Garnish with a few strips of pepper and serve.

La Grande Flouffe

SERVES 6
PREPARATION: 30 MINUTES
COOKING: 5 MINUTES
CHILLING: 1 HOUR

- 1kg (2lb 4oz) black plums, stones discarded
- 2 tablespoons caster sugar
- 1 tablespoon blackcurrant cordial
- 500g (1lb 2oz) strawberries, hulled
- splash of grape juice (optional)
- 300g (10½oz) black grapes
- 200g (7oz) mixture of white currants and redcurrants, destemmed
- 250ml (9fl oz) whipping cream
- 3 tablespoons mascarpone cheese
- 6 good meringues, from your local cake shop

This is the French cousin of the English dessert, Eton Mess, which combines cream and meringue to make a soft cushion for a half-cooked, half-raw summer fruit compote. 'Flouffe' is onomatopoeia for the sound this joyful mixture makes when it lands on your plate!

- Cut half the plums into thin slices and set aside.
- Place the other half of the plums in a saucepan with the sugar and a little water. Heat until bubbling, then simmer for 5 minutes to poach them. Once they are soft, blend to a thick purée in the mixer, then add the blackcurrant cordial.
- Blend half the strawberries, then sieve the purée to remove the seeds. Mix both purées together, adding a splash of grape juice if the mixture is too thick. Leave it to cool completely in the refrigerator.
- Before serving, mix the reserved plum slices with the grapes and currants. Whip the cream and mascarpone together until fairly firm.
- Arrange the meringues on a large dish and spread the cream on top of them. Arrange the fruit on top of the cream and pour over the plum and strawberry sauce. Serve immediately.

Almond blancmanger

SERVES 6
PREPARATION: 20 MINUTES
CHILLING: 4 HOURS

- 400ml (14fl oz) whole milk
- 200ml (7fl oz) double cream
- 50g (1¾oz) caster sugar
- 2 gelatine leaves
- 25g (1oz) ground almonds
- 1 teaspoon bitter almond extract
- handful of chopped pistachios, to serve

- Pour the milk, cream and sugar into a saucepan and bring to the boil. Meanwhile, soak the gelatine leaves in cold water for 5–10 minutes to soften them.
- Take the milk off the heat, add the ground almonds and leave to infuse for 5 minutes. Squeeze the gelatine dry, then stir into the milk until dissolved.
- Add the almond extract, stir well, then pour the mixture into small glasses or cups. Leave to cool and set in the refrigerator for at least 4 hours.
- Serve chilled, garnished with chopped pistachio nuts.

Floating islands with strawberries

SERVES 6
PREPARATION: 15–20 MINUTES
COOKING: 1½ MINUTES

- 500g (1lb 2oz) very ripe strawberries, hulled
- 50g (1¾oz) icing sugar
- 3 egg whites
- mint leaves (optional)

- Blend the strawberries with half the sugar in a blender until you obtain a smooth coulis. Sieve if desired. Set aside in a cool place.
- Whisk the egg whites with the remaining sugar until stiff.
- Use a large spoon to make 'islands' and place them on a plate in batches of three. Put the plate in the microwave for around 15 seconds at 700/800W, keeping a close eye on them! When you see the islands start to rise, remove immediately.
- Leave them to cool completely before serving in bowls surrounded by strawberry coulis. Garnish with a mint leaf if you like.

CHAMPAGNE
CHARLES-HEIDSIECK

Unpredictable weather

Having lunch outside is a risky business, so it's up to you to make sure your guests are comfortable throughout the meal.

In between seasons, provide cushions and blankets for chilly bottoms and knees. One (or two) braziers next to the table is always a good idea, and it means people can get up to chat with others and warm up at the same time.

On very hot days, putting the table under trees, if you can, is the ideal solution. But don't forget that the shade will move around during those long, lazy lunches, so set up one or two small parasols or a large tilting one. Providing hats (and even sun cream) and having fans for people to use are nice ideas for those lunches in the middle of the countryside or large gardens.

If your table isn't under a rainproof shelter, consider half prepping a table inside too, where you can quickly move everything in the event of a downpour.

My second summer menu uses softer, more pastel colours and flavours, giving pride of place to seasonal fruits. I simply serve them as they are, often with a sprinkling of fresh herbs, to celebrate their extraordinary taste at this time of year.

When it is sweltering outside, people tend to eat less, so I often rely on a good fresh goats' cheese board for those guests whose appetites remain intact.

Chilled melon and tarragon soup

SERVES 6–8
PREPARATION: 15 MINUTES
CHILLING: 45–60 MINUTES

- 3 large, ripe charentais or cantaloupe melons
- 1 sprig of fresh tarragon
- ice cubes
- sea salt flakes
- white pepper

- Halve and deseed the melons, then scoop the flesh into a blender. Add the tarragon leaves and blend until smooth.
- Put the soup in the refrigerator for about 1 hour, until it is thoroughly chilled.
- Just before serving, whizz it again in the blender with some ice cubes so that it is really cold. That makes all the difference!
- Season with a sprinkling of sea salt flakes and white pepper just before serving.

Crisp appetizer breads

Following the same 'be prepared' principle as for the go-to tartines on page 233, here are two recipes that can be made quickly for a filling addition to your summer lunches. You'll find ready-made pizza dough or focaccia dough almost everywhere, and it can be stored in the refrigerator until needed.

SERVES 6–8
PREPARATION: 10 MINUTES
COOKING: 25 MINUTES

- olive oil
- 2 shallots, peeled and thinly sliced
- 50ml (2fl oz) white wine
- 200g (7oz) thick crème fraîche
- 200g (7oz) fromage frais
- 1 tablespoon grated Parmesan cheese
- 1 pack ready-made pizza dough or focaccia dough
- 6–8 anchovies in vinegar or salt
- handful of black olives
- salt and pepper

CREAM, ANCHOVY AND OLIVE BREAD

- Preheat the oven to 200°C (400°F), Gas Mark 6.
- Heat a little oil in a frying pan and sweat the shallots, without browning, until soft and translucent. Deglaze the pan with the wine and cook until the liquid has almost evaporated. Set the pan aside.
- Mix the crème fraîche with the fromage frais. Season with salt and pepper, then add the Parmesan.
- Place the dough on a baking tray. Spread the cream over it, then arrange the shallots, anchovies and olives on top. Bake for around 20 minutes, until the edges of the dough are crisp and golden brown and the cream is bubbling gently. Slice and serve hot or warm.

SERVES 6–8
PREPARATION: 5 MINUTES
COOKING: 25 MINUTES

- 4 tomatoes
- 2 shallots, peeled and finely chopped
- 2 garlic cloves, peeled and finely chopped
- olive oil
- 1 tablespoon chopped thyme
- 1 tablespoon chopped rosemary
- 1 tablespoon sun-dried tomato pureé
- small handful of salted capers
- 1 pack ready-made pizza dough or focaccia dough
- 1 tablespoon red onion pickles (see page 22)

TOMATO, CAPER AND ONION PICKLE BREAD

- Preheat the oven to 200°C (400°F), Gas Mark 6.
- Plunge the tomatoes in boiling water for 2 minutes. Let them cool for 30 seconds, then peel off the skin with a knife, and chop the flesh.
- Fry the shallots and garlic in a little olive oil for 1–2 minutes over a medium heat. Add the tomatoes, herbs and sun-dried tomato pureé and let it simmer for 2 minutes until the mixture thickens. Add the capers and set aside.
- Place the dough on baking tray. Spread the tomato mixture over it. Bake for about 20 minutes, until the edges of the dough are crisp and golden, and the topping is bubbling gently. Garnish with onion pickles, then slice and serve hot or warm.

Rainbow tomato carpaccio

SERVES 6
PREPARATION: 10 MINUTES

- 3 large tomatoes of various sizes and colours (yellow, green, orange), at room temperature
- superior-quality olive oil, for drizzling
- chive and/or thyme and/or rosemary flowers
- sea salt flakes
- white pepper

- Slice the tomatoes very thinly and arrange them slightly overlapping on one or two large plates.
- Drizzle over some olive oil, sprinkle with herb flowers and season with salt and white pepper just before serving.

Sardines au gratin with summer vegetables

SERVES 6–8
PREPARATION: 15 MINUTES
COOKING: 10–15 MINUTES

- 2 garlic cloves, peeled and finely chopped
- 3 shallots, peeled and finely chopped
- 1 yellow pepper, deseeded and finely diced
- 1 red pepper, deseeded and finely diced
- 2 courgettes, finely diced
- a sprinkle of thyme leaves and rosemary leaves
- olive oil
- 1 teaspoon grated lemon zest
- 12–16 sardines, gutted and heads removed (ask your fishmonger to clean and behead the fish)
- salt and pepper

- Place the garlic and shallots in a bowl and mix in the rest of the vegetables and herbs, a little olive oil and the lemon zest. Set aside to rest.
- Preheat the oven to 220°C (425°F), Gas Mark 7. Grease an oven tray, or line with a silicone mat.
- Stuff each sardine with the vegetable filling, then place the sardines tightly packed together on the baking tray. Drizzle over a few drops of olive oil and bake for 10–15 minutes, until the skin of the sardines is slightly crisp.
- Remove from the oven, season and serve hot, warm or cold.

Keeping insects away

My kitchen is full of all kinds of food cloches to protect my food in summer. There are often inexpensive ones in the summer collections at Zara Home or H&M. But in France, hunting down antique glass or rattan cloches in vintage shops is always fun. You can also usually find some nice antique glass fly traps to catch greedy wasps.

For a natural way to keep flies and mosquitoes away, put potted mint, basil, lavender or citronella near your table. A few drops of essential oil is also an excellent repellent.

Always keep something on hand to disinfect and relieve wasp, hornet or bee stings.

Fontainebleau minute à la rose

SERVES 6–8
PREPARATION: 5 MINUTES
CHILLING: 1–2 HOURS

- 300ml (10fl oz) whipping cream
- 400g (14oz) soft cheese
- 50g (1¾oz) icing sugar
- a few drops of rosewater

- Beat the cream using an electric whisk.
- Mix the soft cheese with the icing sugar until soft, then fold it into the cream along with a few drops of rosewater.
- Chill for 1–2 hours. Serve with red fruit.

Strawberry and fromage frais tart

SERVES 6–8
PREPARATION: 20 MINUTES
CHILLING: 1 HOUR
COOKING: 25 MINUTES

- 300–400g (10½–14oz) fresh strawberries, hulled and sliced lengthways
- herb flowers

FOR THE PASTRY

- 300g (10½oz) plain flour, plus extra for dusting
- 75g (2¾oz) icing sugar
- 150g (5½oz) very cold unsalted butter, cut into small cubes
- 1 egg, beaten

FOR THE CREAM

- 50g (1¾oz) icing sugar (less if you prefer)
- 350g (12oz) fromage frais, whipped
- seeds from 1 vanilla pod

Based on the same principle as a the raspberry tart on page 264, this recipe has a lighter and tangier filling.

- Start with the pastry. Using your hands or a stand mixer, mix the flour with the icing sugar and butter to obtain a grainy mixture. Mix in the egg, form a dough, then roll into a ball, pressing down on the mixture. Wrap in clingfilm and leave in the refrigerator for about 1 hour.
- Preheat the oven to 180°C (350°F), Gas Mark 4.
- Lightly flour a cold, smooth surface, then roll out the pastry and use it to line your tin (one about 24cm/9½in is ideal). Prick the base of the pastry with a fork, then line the whole pastry case with baking paper. Fill it with ceramic beans (or pulses) and bake blind for 15–20 minutes: the pastry should be golden brown around the edges.
- Lift out the paper and beans, then bake the pastry for a further 5 minutes so that the base is also cooked through. Set aside cool.
- Put the fromage frais and icing sugar in a bowl and mix in the vanilla seeds.
- Assemble the tart just before serving: spread the cold vanilla-flavoured cream inside the pastry case and smooth it over. Arrange the strawberries nicely on top and decorate with the herb flowers. Serve immediately.

TIP

If you want to serve the tart out of the tin, you can line the tin with strips of baking paper that overhang the sides before lining it with the pastry. This will make it easier to lift out.

Peach clafoutis

SERVES 6
PREPARATION: 10 MINUTES
COOKING: 30 MINUTES

- 3 eggs
- 3 tablespoons plain flour
- 3 tablespoons caster sugar, plus extra for sprinkling
- 1 sachet (7–8g) vanilla sugar (or ½ teaspoon vanilla paste or seeds from ½ vanilla pod)
- 2 teaspoons baking powder
- 250–300ml (9–10fl oz) whole milk
- knob of butter
- 4 or 5 peaches (depending on size)

This is less a recipe and more a note to self! It's a wonderful way to transform summer fruits into a dessert that everyone will love.

- Preheat the oven to 180°C (350°F), Gas Mark 4. Grease a 24cm (9½in) gratin dish or cake tin.
- Place all the ingredients, except the peaches, in your mixer bowl and beat them until you have a smooth batter.
- Peel the fruit, if you like. Cut into fairly thick slices. Place them in the dish or tin and then pour the batter around them. Sprinkle on a little extra sugar and bake for around 30 minutes. The clafoutis should be golden brown and puffed up.
- Serve hot, warm or cold.

Raspberry and pistachio tart

SERVES 6–8
PREPARATION: 25 MINUTES
COOKING: 20 MINUTES
CHILLING: 1 HOUR

- 1 quantity chilled shortcrust pastry (see page 260)
- flour, for dusting
- 300–400g (10½–14oz) fresh raspberries

FOR THE PISTACHIO-FLAVOURED CRÈME PÂTISSIÈRE

- 500ml (18fl oz) whole milk
- 1 vanilla pod
- 4 egg yolks
- 70g (2½oz) caster sugar
- 20g (¾oz) cornflour
- 2 tablespoons pistachio paste (sweetened)

- To prepare the crème pâtissière: put the milk in a pan, scrape in the vanilla seeds and add the split pod too, then bring to the boil. Meanwhile, beat the egg yolks in a bowl with the sugar and cornflour until the mixture turns pale and doubles in volume. Remove the vanilla pod from the pan and pour the hot milk over the eggs, stirring constantly with a spatula or wooden spoon.
- Leave to cool for a few minutes before adding the pistachio paste. Stir gently to mix it in thoroughly and enjoy the lovely green colour that appears! Cover with clingfilm to prevent a skin from forming and cool completely in the refrigerator.
- Preheat the oven to 180°C (350°F), Gas Mark 4.
- Lightly flour a cold, smooth surface, then roll out the pastry and use it to line your tin (one about 24cm/9½in is ideal). Prick the base of the pastry with a fork, then line the whole pastry case with baking paper. Fill it with ceramic beans (or pulses) and bake blind for 15–20 minutes: the pastry should be golden brown around the edges.
- Lift out the paper and beans, then bake the pastry for a further 5 minutes so that the base is also cooked through. Set aside cool.
- To assemble the tart, spread the pistachio cream inside the pastry case and smooth it out. Arrange the raspberries tightly packed together on top of the cream, with their open sides facing upwards. Sprinkle with icing sugar and serve.

Our furry friends

Warning! Tricky territory… As with bringing up children, people's methods and ideas about training animals often differ hugely. This could not only ruin a peaceful lunch but also create lasting tensions between friends.

The leg of Great Aunt Alice's armchair gnawed? Kids running barefoot around in the garden accidentally treading on little doggy gifts left in the grass the weekend before? Christmas turkey ripped to bits by brother-in-law's labrador five minutes before sitting down to eat? Historic grudges can cut as deep as a three-year-old doberman's canines.

It is a commonly held belief that people resemble their dogs so, theoretically, if we like our guests, we should like their dogs too (as per the 1970 Peter Shelley song, 'Love Me, Love My Dog'). However, if your dog hasn't been properly trained, it might be best to leave it at home.

Here are three golden rules that help to ensure harmony between species and a peaceful lunch:

- Before arriving with your dog, always check that doing so is okay with everyone. This means any other animals in the house, as well as the hosts and guests who may have allergies or a fear of dogs. (That said, anyone who simply states 'I don't like dogs' is possibly more a prickly character than a valid reason for banning Clementine's very discreet Bedlington whippet.)
- Always bring something to clean up after your dog.
- If your dog is aggressive or gets over-excited in company, it's up to you to calm it down and/or move it away, not up to other dogs to adapt. And just like other people's children, never reprimand a difficult dog that is not yours.

Remember too – a dog begging for food is not pleasant, especially if it is whining or drooling at your knees.

Allowing a dog to eat on your lap or directly from your plate on the table is only for cute puppies or very small dogs belonging to very good friends.

Stealing food is a red card offence!

Index

Index

81276
20084

I dedicate this book to my children, Corentin, Timothée, Tanguy and Victoire, dreaming of all our lovely, tasty lunches to come.

Love you.

All my thanks to:

Catherine Saunier-Talec, Lisa Grall, Joann Pai, Pauline Brunel-Valensi, Hélène Huret, Sophie Feuillade, Jack, Jacqueline and Junon (RIP), Béatrice and Michel Robin, Mona Duveau and José Esteves, Franck and Cécile Schmitt, Laure de Bayser, Carine Pechavy and Armand Wagner.

Useful addresses

A LOVELY GÎTE IN LE PERCHE
La Petite Gaulardière, lapetitegaulardiere.com

CANDLES
Maison Pechavy, maisonpechavy.com

SILICON CHRISTMAS LOG MOULD
cecoa-paris.com

OLD CROCKERY
assiettes-anciennes.fr

COLLECTIONS FOR THE HOME
studio7avril.com

Trish Deseine
trishdeseinefrance.substack.com
trishdeseinefrance.com
@trishdeseineencore

Glossary of UK/US Terms

UK	US
Baking paper	Baking parchment
Celeriac	Celery root
Chickpeas	Garbanzo beans
Clingfilm	Plastic wrap
Cornflour	Cornstarch
Courgette	Zucchini
Cream, single/double	Cream, light/heavy
Dark chocolate	Semi-sweet chocolate
Flaked almonds	Slivered almonds
Flour, plain	Flour, all-purpose
Frying pan	Skillet
Grated	Shredded
Ground almonds	Almond meal
Kitchen paper	Paper towel
Minced pork	Ground pork
Pepper (red)	Bell pepper
Spring onion	Scallion
Stock	Broth
Sugar, caster/icing	Sugar, superfine/confectioners'

First published in Great Britain in 2026 by Kyle Books,
an imprint of Octopus Publishing Group Ltd
Carmelite House
50 Victoria Embankment
London EC4Y 0DZ
www.octopusbooks.co.uk

An Hachette UK Company
www.hachette.co.uk

The authorized representative in the EEA is Hachette Ireland,
8 Castlecourt Centre, Dublin 15, D15 XTP3, Ireland (email: info@hbgi.ie)

Originally published in France in 2024 by Hachette Livre (Hachette Pratique),
58, rue Jean Bleuzen – 92178 Vanves Cedex.

This edition 2026.

Distributed in the US by Hachette Book Group
1290 Avenue of the Americas, 4th and 5th Floors
New York, NY 10104

Distributed in Canada by Canadian Manda Group
664 Annette St., Toronto, Ontario, Canada M6S 2C8

ISBN: 978-1-80419-433-1
eISBN: 978-1-80419-437-9

A CIP catalogue record for this book is available from the British Library.

Printed and bound in China.

10 9 8 7 6 5 4 3 2 1

French edition:
Director: Catherine Saunier-Talec
Editorial manager: Lisa Grall
Editor: Maïa Biegatch
Artistic director: Nicolas Gallois
Food props and styling: Trish Deseine
Production: Amélie Latsch
Partnerships manager: Dana Lichiardopol (dlichiardopol@hachette-livre.fr)

English edition:
Publisher: Joanna Copestick
Editor: Scarlet Furness
Translator: Andrea Reece
Copy editor: Vicky Orchard
Art director: Yasia Williams
Page layout: Jeremy Tilston